BIG
NEEDLE
KNITTING™

Edited by Bobbie Matela

Exclusively using Plymouth yarns

HOUSE of
WHITE
BIRCHES

PUBLISHERS
SINCE 1947

Big Needle Knitting

Copyright © 2005 House of White Birches, Berne, Indiana 46711

EDITOR	Bobbie Matela
ASSOCIATE EDITORS	Mary Ann Frits, Dianne Schmidt, Kathy Wesley
COPY EDITORS	Beverly Richardson, Judy Weatherford
PHOTOGRAPHY	Tammy Christian, Carl Clark, Christena Green, Matthew Owen
PHOTO STYLIST	Tammy Nussbaum
ART DIRECTOR	Brad Snow
PRODUCTION MANAGER	Brenda Gallmeyer
GRAPHIC ARTS SUPERVISOR	Ronda Bechinski
GRAPHIC ARTIST	Adam Rothenberger
PRODUCTION ASSISTANT	Marj Morgan
TECHNICAL ARTIST	Nicole Gage
CHIEF EXECUTIVE OFFICER	John Robinson
PUBLISHING DIRECTOR	David J. McKee
BOOK MARKETING DIRECTOR	Dan Fink

Printed in the United States of America
First printing 2005, China
Library of Congress Number: 2005933235
Hardcover ISBN-10: 1-59217-099-4
Hardcover ISBN-13: 978-1-59217-099-9
Softcover ISBN-10: 1-59217-110-9
Softcover ISBN-13: 978-1-59217-110-1

3 4 5 6 7 8 9

WELCOME

Knitting with big needles is for those who enjoy quick results without sacrificing good looks. Each design in this book is knit on needles that are size 10 or larger. All the yarns, from classic worsted styles to interesting textures and novelty looks, are from the Plymouth Yarn Company.

We put these wonderful yarns in the hands of the most talented designers, and they became the creative medium for the outstanding projects you'll find on these pages. You will enjoy making, wearing and giving great-looking designs that don't take forever to make.

Fulfill your nesting instincts with afghans, throws, pillows and rugs that will surround you and your loved ones in warmth and cozy style.

If, like most knitters, sweaters are your favorite pastime, we've included a chapter of super sweater styles for the whole family—even the family dog. You'll find innovative looks for man, woman and child.

You'll also find irresistible wraps including ponchos, capes, shawls and a ruana. These are the kind of wraps that are enjoyed by all ages. We've even included a young girl's poncho.

If you're looking for gifts that you can actually complete when time is limited, big needle is definitely the way to go. Our final chapter has an array of quick accessory ideas from scarves and purses to hats and mittens.

We're sure you'll enjoy this collection and how productive you'll be with your big needles!

Warm regards,

Bobbie Matela

CONTENTS

Inviting Home

Warm Family

Stylish Wraps

Hurry Up Gifts

INVITING HOME

It's fun to add color, warmth and texture to your bedroom and living areas with big-needle hand-knit throws, pillows and rugs.

TRADING POST RUG & PILLOW

Design by Pauline Schultz

Add a Southwest touch to your decor with a matching rug and cushion.

SIZE
Rug: Approx 28 x 58 inches
Pillow: 24 x 24 inches

SKILL LEVEL
EXPERIENCED

YARN WEIGHT
6
SUPER BULKY

MATERIALS
Rug
- Plymouth Encore Mega 75 percent acrylic/25 percent wool super bulky weight yarn (64 yds/100g per skein): 3 skeins each black #217 (A), charcoal gray #389 (B), oatmeal #240 (C), maroon #999 (D)
- Size 15 (10mm) 29-inch circular needle or size needed to obtain gauge

Pillow
- Plymouth Encore Mega 75 percent acrylic/25 percent wool super bulky weight yarn (64 yds/100g per skein): 3 skeins black #217 (A), 2 skeins charcoal gray #389 (B), 1 skein oatmeal #240 (C), 2 skeins maroon #999 (D)
- Size 15 (10mm) 29-inch circular

needle or size needed to obtain gauge
• 24-inch square purchased pillow form

GAUGE

8 sts and 16 rows = 4 inches/10cm in garter st

To save time, take time to check gauge.

PATTERN NOTES

Circular needle is used to accommodate heavy yarn. Do not join; work in rows.

Rug is knit in one piece using bobbins and intarsia method.

Refer to diagrams for color placement in blocks.

Pillow consists of 2 large blocks.

Wind separate balls or bobbins for each color area.

To avoid holes when changing colors, always bring new color up over old.

Rug

BASIC BLOCK PATTERN

Rows 1–6: Knit with first color.

Rows 7–12: K3 with first color, k11 with 2nd color, k3 with first color.

Rows 13–20: K3 with first color, k3 with 2nd color, k5 with 3rd

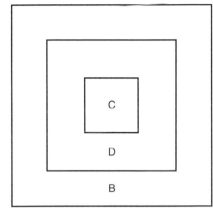

Trading Post Rug
Block 1

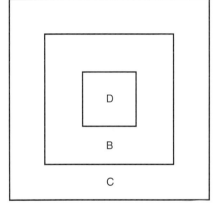

Trading Post Rug
Block 2

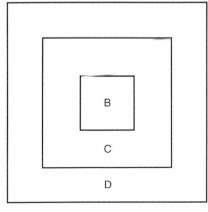

Trading Post Rug
Block 3

color, k3 with 2nd color, k3 with first color.

Rows 21–26: Rep Rows 7–12.

Rows 27–32: Rep Rows 1–6.

RUG INSTRUCTIONS

With A cast on 57 sts.
Knit 6 rows.

Set up pat

Using basic block k3A, work Row 1 of block 1 over 17 sts, Row 1 of block 2 over 17 sts, Row 1 of block 3 over 17 sts, k3 A.

Continue in established color sequence until 32 rows of blocks have been completed.

Knit 6 rows A.

Referring to photo and having 6 rows of A between each row of blocks, continue to work as established until 6 rows of blocks have been completed.

Knit 6 rows A.
Bind off.

Pillow

PILLOW A
(shown on pages 9 and 11)

With A, cast on 50 sts.

Knit 10 rows.

Rows 1–14: K6 A, k38 D, k6 A.

Rows 15–28: K6 A, k7 D, k24 C, k7 D, k6 A.

Rows 29–48: K6 A, k7 D, k7 C, k10 B, k7 C, k7 D, k6 A.

Rows 49–62: Rep Rows 15–28.

Rows 63–76: Rep Rows 1–14.
Knit 10 Rows A.
Bind off.

PILLOW B (shown on page 8)

With A, cast on 50 sts.
Knit 10 rows.

Rows 1–14: K6 A, k38 C, k6 A.

Rows 15–28: K6 A, k7 C, k24 B, k7 C, k6 A.

Rows 29–48: K6 A, k7 C, k7 B, k10 D, k7 B, k7 C, k6 A.

Rows 49–62: Rep Rows 15–28.

Rows 63–76: Rep Rows 1–14.
Knit 10 Rows A.
Bind off.

ASSEMBLY

With WS tog, sew 3 sides of blocks. Insert pillow form; sew rem side. ∎

MAKE MINE COLORFUL THROW

Design by Kennita Tully

Openwork and ribs give a slightly different appearance to each side of a reversible throw.

SIZE
Approx 48 x 58 inches

SKILL LEVEL
EASY

YARN WEIGHT
6
SUPER BULKY

MATERIALS
• Plymouth Yukon Print 35 percent wool/35 percent mohair/30 percent acrylic super bulky weight yarn (60 yds/100g per skein): 15 skeins pastel print #2010

• Size 15 (10mm) 29-inch circular needle or size needed to obtain gauge

GAUGE
9 sts and 9 rows = 4 inches/10cm in Double Lace Rib pat

To save time, take time to check gauge.

PATTERN STITCH
Double Lace Rib
Row 1 (RS): K3, *p1, yo, k2tog-tbl, p1, k2; rep from * to last st, k1.
Row 2: P3, *k1, p2; rep from * to last st, p1.
Row 3: K3, *p1, k2tog, yo, p1, k2; rep from * to last st, k1.
Row 4: Rep Row 2.
Rep Rows 1–4 for pat.

PATTERN NOTE
Circular needle is used to accommodate large number of sts.
Do not join; work in rows.

THROW
Cast on 106 sts.
Beg with Row 2 of pat, work even in pat for approx 58 inches, ending with Row 1.
Bind off in pat. ∎

TROPICAL PARADISE THROW & PILLOW

Design by Anita Closic

Tropical colors and feathery yarn will add an island touch to your decor.

SIZE
Throw: Approx 48 x 60 inches
Pillow: Approx 12 x 12 inches

SKILL LEVEL
EASY
YARN WEIGHT
6 SUPER BULKY

MATERIALS
Throw
- Plymouth Rimini Rainbow 60 percent acrylic/40 percent wool super bulky weight yarn (38 yds/50g per ball): 8 balls rainbow greens #20 (A)
- Plymouth Jungle 100 percent nylon super bulky weight yarn (61 yds/50g per ball): 4 balls tropical #1 (B)
- Plymouth Parrot 100 percent nylon (28 yds/50g per ball): 5 balls tropical variegated #1 (C)
- Size 15 (10mm) 32-inch circular needle or size needed to obtain gauge

Pillow
- Plymouth Rimini Rainbow 60 percent acrylic/40 percent wool super bulky weight yarn (38 yds/50g per ball): 2 balls rainbow greens #20 (A)
- Plymouth Jungle 100 percent nylon super bulky weight yarn (61 yds/50g per ball): 2 balls tropical #1 (B)

- Plymouth Parrot 100 percent nylon (28 yds/50g per ball): 2 balls tropical variegated #1 (C)
- Size 15 (10mm) straight needles or size needed to obtain gauge
- 1 (12 x 12-inch) purchased pillow form
- Size K/10½/6.5mm crochet hook

GAUGE
Throw: 8 sts and 10 rows = 4 inches/10cm in Openwork pat
Pillow: 8 sts and 14 rows = 4 inches/10cm in pat sequence
To save time, take time to check gauge.

PATTERN STITCH
Openwork Pattern
All rows: K2, *yo, K2tog; rep from * to last 2 sts, k2.

PATTERN NOTES
Circular needle is used to accommodate large number of sts.
Do not join; work in rows.

Throw

With circular needle and B, cast on 96 sts.
Knit 2 rows.
Rows 1 and 2: With C, knit.
Rows 3–6: With B, knit.
Rows 7–16: With A, work in Openwork pat.
Rows 17–20: With C, knit.
Rows 21 and 22: With B, knit.
Rows 23 and 24: With B, work in Openwork pat.
Rep [Rows 1–24] 6 times.
Rep Rows 1–22.
Bind off loosely.

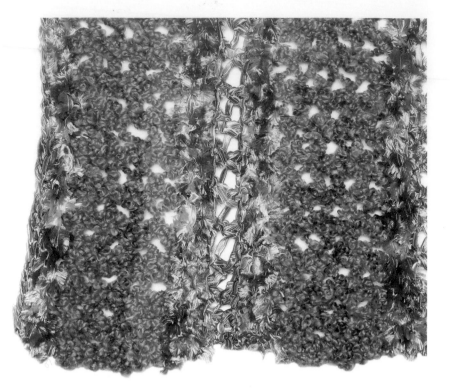

Pillow

FRONT/BACK
With straight needle and B, cast on 24 sts.
Knit 2 rows.
Rows 1–4: With C, knit.
Rows 5–8: With A, work in Openwork pat.
Rows 9–12: With C, knit.
Rows 13 and 14: With B, work in Openwork pat.
Rep [Rows 1–14] twice.
Rep Rows 1–12. Knit 2 rows.
Bind off loosely.

ASSEMBLY
Note: *If not familiar with single crochet, refer to page 173.*
With B, sc pillow tops tog along 3 sides; do not cut yarn.

Insert pillow form; work sc along rem side.

EDGING
Working from left to right, work 1 row of sc in each sc around.
Join with sl st and fasten off.

TASSELS
Make 4
Cut 4 lengths of C, each 10 inches long.
Holding strands tog, fold group in half.
Insert crochet hook from WS to RS in corner st.
Pull fold of tassel through corner of throw. Draw ends through lp and fasten tightly.
Rep for rem corners.
Trim tassels evenly. ■

TWIST THE NIGHT AWAY AFGHAN

Design by Laura Polley

Handsome cables and ribs combine to create a heavily textured afghan. The reverse side is equally pleasant looking.

SIZE
Approx 50 x 55 inches

SKILL LEVEL
INTERMEDIATE

YARN WEIGHT
4
MEDIUM

MATERIALS
- Plymouth Galway Colornep 93 percent wool/7 percent polyester worsted weight yarn (210 yds/100g per skein): 27 skeins green tweed #527
- Size 15 (10mm) 29-inch circular needle or size needed to obtain gauge
- Stitch markers
- Cable needle

GAUGE
16 sts and 14 rows = 4 inches/10cm in Tweed Twist pat with 3 strands of yarn held tog

To save time, take time to check gauge.

SPECIAL ABBREVIATIONS
M1 (Make 1): Make a backward lp and place on RH needle.

C4F (Cable 4 Front): Sl 2 sts to cn and hold in front of work, k2, k2 from cn.

C4B (Cable 4 Back): Sl 2 sts to cn and hold in back of work, k2, k2 from cn.

T3F (Twist 3 Front): Sl 2 sts to cn and hold in front of work, p1, k2 from cn.

T3B (Twist 3 Back): Sl 1 st to cn and hold in back of work, k2, p1 from cn.

PATTERN STITCHES

Moss
Rows 1 (RS) and 2: *K1, p1; rep from * across.
Rows 3 and 4: *P1, k1; rep from * across.
Rep Rows 1–4 for pat.

Tweed Twist
Row 1 (RS): K3, p2, k2, p2, *k6, p2, k2, p2; rep from * to last 3 sts, k3.
Row 2: P3, k2, p2, k2, *p6, k2, p2, k2; rep from * to last 3 sts, p3.
Row 3: K3, p2, k2, p2, *C4F, [k2, p2] twice; rep from * to last 3 sts, k3.
Row 4: Rep Row 2.
Row 5: K1, T3F, p1, k2, p1, T3B, *k2, T3F, p1, k2, p1, T3B; rep from * to last st, k1.
Row 6: P1, k1, *p2, k1; rep from * to last st, k1.
Row 7: K1, p1, T3F, k2, T3B, p1, *k2, p1, T3F, k2, T3B, p1; rep from * to last st, k1.
Row 8: P1, k2, p6, k2, *p2, k2, p6, k2; rep from * to last st, p1.
Row 9: K1, p2, k2, C4B, *[p2, k2] twice, C4B; rep from * to last 3 sts, p2, k1.
Row 10: Rep Row 8.
Row 11: K1, p2, k6, p2, *k2, p2, k6, p2; rep from * to last st, k1.
Row 12: Rep Row 8.
Row 13: K1, p2, C4F, *[k2, p2] twice, C4F; rep from * to last 5 sts, k2, p2, k1.
Row 14: Rep Row 8.
Row 15: K1, p1, T3B, k2, T3F, p1, *k2, p1, T3B, k2, T3F, p1; rep from * to last st, k1.
Row 16: Rep Row 6.
Row 17: K1, T3B, p1, k2, p1, T3F, *k2, p1, T3B, p1, k2, p1, T3F; rep from * to last st, k1.
Row 18: Rep Row 2.
Row 19: K3, [p2, k2] twice, *C4B, [p2, k2] twice; rep from * to last st, k1.
Row 20: Rep Row 2.
Rep Rows 1–20 for pat.

PATTERN NOTES
Circular needle is used to accommodate large number of sts.
Do not join; work in rows.
Afghan is worked holding 3 strands of yarn tog throughout.

AFGHAN
With 3 strands of yarn held tog, cast on 136 sts.
Work 5 rows in Moss pat.
Inc row (WS): Work 4 sts in Moss pat, M1, k1, *M1, work 3 sts in Moss pat; rep from * to last 5 sts, M1, k1, work 4 sts in Moss pat. (180 sts)
Next row: Work Moss pat as established over first 6 sts, pm, work Row 1 of Tweed Twist pat over center 168 sts, pm, work Moss pat as established over last 6 sts.
Keeping first and last 6 sts in Moss pat, and sts between markers in Tweed Twist pat, work even until afghan measures approx 53½ inches from beg, ending with Row 20 of Tweed Twist pat.
Dec row (RS): K1, p1, k1, p2tog, *k1, p1, k2tog, p1, k1, p2tog; rep from * to last 3 sts, k1, p1, k1. (136 sts)
Removing markers, work 5 rows in Moss pat over all sts.
Bind off loosely in pat. ■

OVER OR UNDER REVERSIBLE AFGHAN

Design by Lois S. Young

Each side of this cozy afghan presents a different texture. Easy stitches create the effect.

SIZE
Approx 42 x 56 inches

SKILL LEVEL
■■□□
EASY

YARN WEIGHT
6
SUPER BULKY

MATERIALS
- Plymouth Yukon 35 percent mohair/35 percent wool/30 percent acrylic super bulky weight yarn (59 yds/100g per skein): 17 skeins red heather #89
- Size 15 (10mm) 29-inch circular needle or size needed to obtain gauge
- Size M/13/9mm crochet hook

GAUGE
9½ sts and 14 rows = 4 inches/ 10cm in pat st
    To save time, take time to check gauge.

PATTERN STITCH
Over or Under
Rows 1, 3, 5 and 7 (Curved Ribbing Side): Sl 1, k2, *k5, p3; rep from * to last 8 sts, k8.
Rows 2, 4, 6 and 8 (Woven Blocks Side): Sl 1, k2, *[p1, k1] twice, p1, k3; rep from * across.

Rows 9, 11, 13 and 15: Sl 1, k3, *p3, k5; rep from * to last 7 sts, p3, k4.
Rows 10, 12, 14 and 16: Sl 1, k2, *p1, k3, [p1, k1] twice; rep from * to last 8 sts, [p1, k3],twice.
    Rep Rows 1–16 for pat.

PATTERN NOTES
Circular needle is used to accommodate large number of sts. Do not join; work in rows. Sl first st of each row purlwise wyif.

AFGHAN

Cast on 99 sts.

Next row: Sl 1p wyif, knit across.

Rep [Rows 1–16 of Over or Under pat] 22 times.

Rep Rows 1–8 of Over or Under pat.

Next row: Sl 1p wyif, knit to end of row.

Bind off knitwise, working last 2 sts as k2tog.

FRINGE

Following Fringe instructions on page 173, make Single Knot fringe.

Cut 16-inch strands of yarn.

Holding 3 strands tog, place knots evenly spaced (every 5th st) across cast-on edge.

Rep across bound-off edge.

Trim ends evenly. ■

WOVEN FOR WARMTH AFGHAN

Design by Gayle Bunn

A woven-look pattern and bulky yarn combine to create an afghan you will want to snuggle under next to the fireplace.

SIZE
Approx 48 x 54 inches

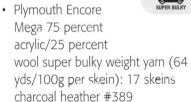

SKILL LEVEL
◼◼◻◻
EASY

YARN WEIGHT
🔶 6
SUPER BULKY

MATERIALS
- Plymouth Encore Mega 75 percent acrylic/25 percent wool super bulky weight yarn (64 yds/100g per skein): 17 skeins charcoal heather #389
- Size 15 (10mm) 36-inch circular needle or size needed to obtain gauge

GAUGE
9 sts and 12 rows = 4 inches/10cm in St st
  To save time, take time to check gauge.

PATTERN STITCHES
Seed
All rows: K1, *p1, k1; rep from * across row.
Woven Blanket
Row 1 (RS): Knit.
Row 2: Purl.

Row 3: K3, *p7, k5; rep from * to last 10 sts, p7, k3.
Row 4: P3, *k7, p5; rep from * to last 10 sts, k7, p3.
Rows 5–8: Rep rows 1–4.
Row 9: Knit.
Row 10: Purl.
Row 11: P4, *k5, p7; rep from * to last 9 sts, k5, p4.
Row 12: K4, *p5, k7; rep from * to last 9 sts, p5, k4.
Rows 13–16: Rep rows 9–12.
  Rep Rows 1–16 for pat.

PATTERN NOTE
Circular needle is used to accommodate large number of sts.
　Do not join; work in rows.

AFGHAN
Cast on 97 sts.
　Work even in Seed pat for 8 rows.
　Change to Woven Blanket pat and work even until afghan measures approx 53 inches, ending with Row 10 of pat.
　Work 8 rows in Seed pat.
　Bind off in pat.

SIDE BORDER
With RS facing, pick up and knit 115 sts evenly along one side edge of afghan.
　Work 7 rows in Seed pat.
　Bind off in pat.
　Rep on opposite side edge. ■

TAKE NOTICE PILLOWS

Design by Lanie Hering

Two coordinating pillows are a perfect project for beginners.

SIZE
Approx 16 x 16 inches

SKILL LEVEL
BEGINNER

YARN WEIGHT
6 SUPER BULKY

MATERIALS
- Plymouth Parrot 100 percent nylon super bulky weight yarn (28 yds/50g per ball): 7 balls brown shades #5 (pillow #1) **or** off-white shades #43 (pillow #2)
- Size 13 (9mm) 29-inch circular needle or size needed to obtain gauge
- Stitch marker
- 1 (16-inch square) purchased pillow form
- Sewing needle and matching thread

GAUGE
9 sts and 14 rows = 4 inches/ 10cm in St st

To save time, take time to check gauge.

PILLOW
Cast on 72 sts. Join without twisting, placing marker between first and last st.

Work even in St st until pillow cover measures 16 inches.

Bind off.

ASSEMBLY
Fold piece in half with WS tog. With matching thread, sew 2 sides tog. Turn cover so RS is facing outward.

Insert pillow form and sew rem edge. ■

EVENING AT HOME THROW

Design by Katharine Hunt

Earthy colors and crossed and slipped-stitch stripes make this an interesting project to knit.

SIZE
Approx 46 x 51 inches

MATERIALS
- Plymouth Encore Worsted 75 percent acrylic/25 percent wool worsted weight yarn (200 yds/100g per skein): 6 skeins each tan/gray heather #1405 (A) and beige heather #1415 (B); 2 skeins each cranberry heather #560 (C) and brown heather #1444 (D)
- Size 11 (8mm) 30-inch circular needle or size needed to obtain gauge
- Cable needle or one double-pointed needle size 11 (8mm) or smaller

GAUGE
11 sts and 11 rows = 4 inches/10cm in garter st with 2 strands of yarn held tog

PATTERN NOTES

Circular needle is used to accommodate large number of sts. Do not join; work in rows. Two strands of yarn are held tog for entire throw. Refer to pat instructions for color combinations.

THROW

With A/B, cast on 136 sts.
*Knit 11 rows.
Work 2 rows of Cross St Stripe pat.
Knit 9 rows.
Work Rows 1–8 of Checked Basket pat.
Knit 9 rows.
Work 2 rows of Cross St Stripe pat.
Knit 9 rows.
Work Rows 1–20 of Checked Basket pat *.
Rep from * to * twice.
Knit 9 rows.
Work 2 rows of Cross St Stripe pat.
Knit 9 rows.
Work Rows 1–8 of Checked Basket pat.
Knit 9 rows.
Work 2 rows of Cross St Stripe pat.
Knit 10 rows.
Bind off knitwise on WS.

FRINGE

Following Fringe instructions on page 170, make Single Knot fringe.
Cut 14-inch strands of A and B. Holding 2 strands each of A and B tog and working across cast-on edge, place knot centered under each Cross St.
Rep across bound-off edge.
Trim ends evenly. ■

To save time, take time to check gauge.

PATTERN STITCHES
Cross Stitch Stripe

Row 1 (WS): *Insert RH needle into next st and wrap yarn twice around needle, knit this stitch drawing all wraps through; rep from * once. Rep from * across row to last 2 sts wrapping yarn 3 times instead of twice; work last 2 sts as first 2.

Row 2: Sl first 2 sts to cn or dpn, dropping wraps. Rotate extra needle clockwise 180 degrees twice, place twisted sts back on LH needle and knit each st. *Sl next 6 sts wyib, dropping extra wraps. Insert tip of LH needle under first 3 of 6 long sts from the left and pass them over 2nd 3 sts and off needle. Return 3 long sts from RH to LH needle and knit them. Pick up first 3 dropped sts and knit them. Rep from * for each set of 6 sts across, to last 2 sts. Work last 2 sts as for first.

Rep Rows 1 and 2 for pat.

Checked Basket

Rows 1 (RS) and 2: With C/D, knit.
Row 3: With A/B, k1, *sl 2 wyib, k4; rep from * to last 3 sts, sl 2, k1.
Row 4: With A/B, k1, *sl 2 wyif, k4; rep from * to last 3 sts, sl 2, k1.
Rows 5 and 6: Rep Rows 3 and 4.
Row 7 and 8: With C/D, knit.
Row 9: With A/B, k4, *sl 2 wyib, k4; rep from * across.
Row 10: With A/B, k4, *sl 2 wyif, k4; rep from * across.
Rows 11 and 12: Rep Rows 9 and 10.
Rows 13–20: Rep Rows 1–8. Rep Rows 1–20 for pat.

EVERYONE LOVES DIAMONDS AFGHAN

Design by Laura Polley

Light and luscious, this lacy afghan is sure to be a summer showstopper!

SIZE
Approx 51 x 56 inches

SKILL LEVEL
■■■□
INTERMEDIATE

YARN WEIGHT
4
MEDIUM

MATERIALS
- Plymouth Fantasy Naturale 100 percent cotton worsted weight yarn (140 yds/100g per skein): 16 skeins sea green #5425
- Size 15 (10mm) 36-inch circular needle or size needed to obtain gauge
- Stitch markers

GAUGE
9½ sts and 14 rows = 4 inches/10cm in Diamond Lace pat
   To save time, take time to check gauge.

PATTERN STITCH
Diamond Lace (multiple of 10 sts + 13)
Row 1 (RS): K2, yo, ssk, k5, k2tog, yo, *k1, yo, ssk, k5, k2tog, yo; rep from * to last 2 sts, k2.
Row 2: P4, k5, *p5, k5; rep from * to last 4 sts, p4.
Row 3: K3, *yo, ssk, k3, k2tog, yo, k3; rep from * across row.
Row 4: P5, k3, *p7, k3; rep from * to last 5 sts, p5.
Row 5: K4, yo, ssk, k1, k2tog, yo, *k5, yo, ssk, k1, k2tog, yo; rep

from * to last 4 sts, k4.

Row 6: P6, k1, *p9, k1; rep from * to last 6 sts, p6.

Row 7: K5, yo, sl 1, k2tog, psso, yo, *k7, yo, sl 1, k2tog, psso, yo; rep from * to last 5 sts, k5.

Row 8: Purl.

Row 9: K4, k2tog, yo, k1, yo, ssk, *k5, k2tog, yo, k1, yo, sl 1, k1, psso; rep from * to last 4 sts, k4.

Row 10: K4, p5, *k5, p5; rep from * to last 4 sts, k4.

Row 11: K3, *k2tog, yo, k3, yo, ssk, k3; rep from * to end.

Row 12: K3, *p7, k3; rep from * across row.

Row 13: K2, k2tog, yo, k5, yo, ssk, *k1, k2tog, yo, k5, yo, ssk; rep from * to last 2 sts, k2.

Row 14: P1, k1, *p9, k1; rep from * to last st, p1.

Row 15: K1, k2tog, yo, k7, *yo, sl 1, k2tog, psso, yo, k7; rep from * to last 3 sts, yo, ssk, k1.

Row 16: Purl.

Rep Rows 1–16 for pat

PATTERN NOTES

Circular needle is used to accommodate large number of sts.

Do not join; work in rows.

Two strands of yarn are held tog for entire afghan.

AFGHAN

With 2 strands of yarn held tog, cast on 111 sts.

Knit 5 rows.

Set up pat (RS): K4, pm, work Row 1 of Diamond Lace pat over next 103 sts, pm, k4.

Keeping sts between markers in Diamond Lace pat and last 4 sts in garter st, work even until afghan measures approx 54 inches from beg, ending with Row 8 of pat.

Knit 5 rows.

Loosely bind off knitwise on WS.■

FLYING COLORS FELTED RUG & PILLOW

Design by Laura Polley

Soft, warm and inviting, these felted beauties will decorate your home in contemporary style!

SIZE

Rug: Approx 36 x 20 inches, not including trim, after felting

Pillow: Approx 30 x 30 inches, not including trim, after felting

SKILL LEVEL
EXPERIENCED

YARN WEIGHT
4 MEDIUM

MATERIALS
RUG

• Plymouth Galway 100 percent wool worsted weight yarn (210 yds/100g per ball): 6 balls purple #132 (A), 3 balls slate blue #128 (C)
• Plymouth Galway Highland Heather 100 percent wool worsted weight yarn (210 yds/100g per ball): 3 balls gold #744 (B)
• Size 15 (10mm) needles or size needed to obtain gauge
• Spray-on rug backing or nonskid pad (optional)

PILLOW

- Plymouth Galway 100 percent wool worsted weight yarn (210 yds/100g per ball): 15 balls purple#132 (A), 6 balls slate blue #128 (C)
- Plymouth Galway Highland Heather 100 percent wool worsted weight yarn (210 yds/ 100g per ball): 6 balls gold #744 (B)
- Size 15 (10mm) needles or size needed to obtain gauge
- 5 (1¼-inch long) toggle buttons
- Purchased pillow form, 30 inches square
- Fine cotton crochet thread to match buttons
- Sewing needle

GAUGE

8½ sts and 12 rows = 4 inches/ 10cm in St st before felting

To save time, take time to check gauge.

SPECIAL ABBREVIATION

M1 (Make 1): Make a backward lp and place on RH needle.

PATTERN NOTES

Projects are worked holding 3 strands of yarn tog throughout.

Intarsia method is used for both projects. To avoid holes when changing colors, always bring new color up over old.

Charts include 1 selvage st each side. These sts will disappear during sewing.

Use mattress st (see page 38) or another flat seam for all sewing, taking in 1 full st from each piece, and using 3 strands of matching yarn.

Rug

PANEL 1

With 3 strands of A held tog, cast on 19 sts.

Work in St st for 6 rows.

Referring to Rug Chart A, rep [Rows 1–34] twice.

Change to A and work in St st for 6 rows.

Bind off.

PANEL 2

With 3 strands of A held tog, cast on 19 sts.

Work in St st for 6 rows.

Referring to Rug Chart B, rep [Rows 1–34] twice.

Change to A and work in St st for 6 rows.

Bind off.

PANEL 3

With 3 strands of A held tog, cast on 19 sts.

Work in St st for 6 rows with A, 68 rows B, 6 rows A.

Bind off.

PANEL 4

With 3 strands of A, cast on 19 sts.

Work in St st for 6 rows.

Referring to Rug Chart C, rep [Rows 1–34] twice.

Change to A and work in St st for 6 rows.

Bind off.

PANEL 5

With 3 strands of A, cast on 19 sts.

Work in St st for 6 rows.

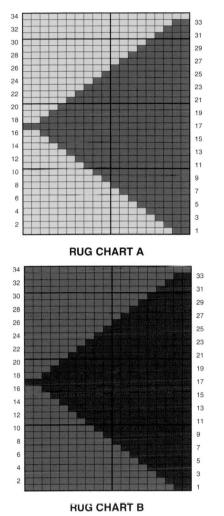

RUG CHART A

RUG CHART C

RUG CHART B

RUG CHART D

COLOR KEY
■ Purple (A)
□ Gold (B)
■ Slate Blue (C)

Weave in all yarn ends.

EDGING
With tapestry needle and double strand of C, work blanket st embroidery *(see illustration)* over top 2 ridges of border around entire outer edge of rug.

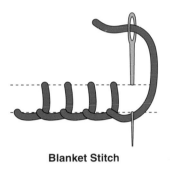

Blanket Stitch

FELTING
Felt according to Felting instruction for Pillow on page 39.

Optional: If desired, apply spray-on rug backing or a nonskid pad to WS of rug to keep rug stationary during use.

Pillow

FRONT
PANEL 1
With 3 strands of A held tog, cast on 16 sts.
Work in St st for 8 rows.
Referring to Pillow Chart A, (on page 38), rep [Rows 1–28] 4 times.
Change to A and work in St st for 8 rows.
Bind off.

PANEL 2
With 3 strands of A held tog, cast on 16 sts.
Work in St st for 8 rows.
Referring to Pillow Chart B (on page 38), rep [Rows 1–28] 4 times.
Change to A and work in St st for 8 rows.

Referring to Rug Chart D, rep [Rows 1–34] twice.
Change to A and work in St st for 6 rows.
Bind off.

SIDE PANELS
Make 2
With 3 strands of A, cast on 5 sts.
Work in St st for 80 rows.
Bind off.

ASSEMBLY
Arrange panels in numerical order from left to right, with a side panel at each side edge.

Sew tog, matching colors.

BORDER
With RS facing using 3 strands of A, pick up and knit 93 sts along upper edge of rug.
Knit 3 rows.
Bind off purlwise on RS.
Rep for lower edge of rug.
With RS facing using 3 strands of A, pick up and knit 60 sts along side edge of rug, including upper and lower trims.
Knit 3 rows.
Bind off purlwise on RS.
Rep for 2nd side edge of rug.

Bind off.

PANEL 3

With 3 strands of A held tog, cast on 16 sts.

Work in St st for 8 rows with A, 112 rows B, 8 rows A.

Bind off.

PANEL 4

With 3 strands of A held tog, cast on 16 sts.

Work in St st for 8 rows.

Referring to Pillow Chart C, (on page 38), rep [Rows 1–28] 4 times.

Change to A and work in St st for 8 rows.

Bind off.

PANEL 5

With 3 strands of A held tog, cast on 16 sts.

Work in St st for 8 rows.

Referring to Pillow Chart D, [rep Rows 1–28] 4 times.

Change to A and work in St st for 8 rows.

Bind off.

SIDE PANELS
Make 2

With 3 strands A held tog, cast on 5 sts.

Work 128 rows in St st.

Bind off.

BACK
SIDE PANELS
Make 2

With 3 strands of A held tog, cast on 33 sts.

Work 128 rows in St st.

Bind off.

BUTTON PANEL

With 3 strands of A held tog, cast on 15 sts.

Work in St st for 8 rows with A, 112 rows B, 8 rows A.

Bind off.

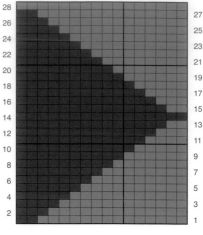

PILLOW CHART A

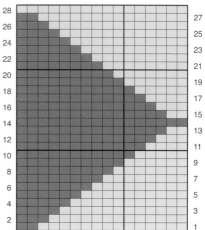

PILLOW CHART C

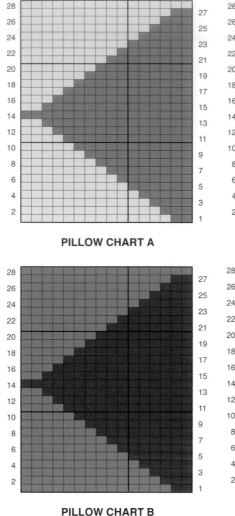

PILLOW CHART B

PILLOW CHART D

COLOR KEY
- ■ Purple (A)
- □ Gold (B)
- ▨ Slate Blue (C)

BUTTONHOLE PANEL

With 3 strands A held tog, cast on 15 sts.

Work in St st for 6 rows.

Make buttonhole

Row 1 (RS): Knit to last 6 sts, bind off 3, k3.

Row 2: P3, cast on 3 sts over bound-off sts by making a backward lp around needle, purl to end of row.

Change to C.

BUTTONHOLE POINTS

Row 1: Knit to last 3 sts, k2tog, k1. (14 sts)

Row 2: P1, p2tog, purl to end of row. (13 sts)

Rows 3–12: Rep Rows 1 and 2. (3 sts)

Row 13: K2tog, k1. (2 sts)

Row 14: Purl.

Row 15: Knit to last st, M1, k1. (3 sts)

Row 16: P1, M1, purl to end of row. (4 sts)

Rows 17–26: Rep Rows 15 and 16. (14 sts)

Row 27: Knit to last 5 sts, bind off 3, k1, M1, k1. (15 sts including bound-off sts)

Row 28: Purl, casting on 3 sts over bound-off sts as for first buttonhole.

Rep [Rows 1–28] twice.

Rep Rows 1–26.

Rep Row 15.

Next row: Purl.

Change to A.

Rep buttonhole Rows 1 and 2.

Work in St st for 6 rows.

Bind off.

ASSEMBLY

Arrange front panels in numerical order from left to right, with a side border at each side edge.

Sew tog, matching colors.

Sew left half pieces tog, having side panel on left and button panel at right edge.

Sew right half pieces tog, having side panel on right, and buttonhole panel at left.

BORDER

With RS facing, arrange pillow back pieces with buttonhole panel of right half overlapping button panel of left half. Pin in place.

With RS facing using 3 strands of A, pick up and knit 32 sts along upper edge to just before buttonhole panel. Working through both thicknesses of button and buttonhole panels, pick up and knit 14 sts along top of overlapped panels. Pick up and knit 32 sts along remainder of upper edge of pillow. (78 sts)

Knit 3 rows.

Bind off purlwise on RS.

Rep for lower edge, working through both thicknesses of center panels as for upper edge.

With 3 strands of A, pick up and knit 92 sts along side edge of pillow, including upper and lower edgings.

Knit 3 rows.

Bind off purlwise on RS.

Rep for 2nd side edge.

Weave in all yarn ends.

Join front and back

With WS tog, using 3 strands of A, sew front and back pillow pieces tog using a whipstitch or overcast seam, around entire outer edge of pillow.

With double strand of C, work blanket stitch embroidery (*refer to photo and illustration on page 37*) over border around entire outside edge of pillow, working through front thickness of pillow only.

Mark back button panel for five buttons evenly spaced underneath buttonholes.

FELTING

Using sewing needle and cotton thread, loosely baste all around center of each buttonhole, to keep buttonholes open during felting. Use a washing machine set on a low to medium water level. Include one tablespoon of dish detergent or wool shampoo in water. Use the hottest water temperature possible.

Place completed piece in water, along with a pair of faded jeans to increase agitation. Set washer to medium wash time, and allow washer to run just until the water has drained. Do not allow rinse cycle to begin.

Remove piece carefully without stretching, and check measurements.

If it is not shrunk to desired size, wash again as before, without rinsing, and check measurements again.

When approx desired size, block carefully to shape, stretching as necessary along edges. (This must be done while still wet.) Leave in place until dry.

Sew on buttons opposite buttonholes. Insert pillow form and button pillow back closed. ■

WARM FAMILY

Keep them warm with picture-perfect stylish
sweaters. Here are big-needle designs
for everyone—including dad, mom, kids,
baby and even the pampered family pooch!

MOM'S CASUAL CABLE CARDIGAN

Design by Celeste Pinheiro

Bright buttons add a perfect touch to a casual cable and rib cardie for Mom.

SIZE

Woman's small (medium, large, extra-large) Instructions are given for smallest size, with larger sizes in parentheses. When only 1 number is given, it applies to all sizes.

SKILL LEVEL
■■■□ INTERMEDIATE

YARN WEIGHT
(5) BULKY

FINISHED MEASUREMENTS

Chest: 42 (46, 50, 54) inches
Length: 22 (23, 24, 25) inches

MATERIALS

- Plymouth Encore Chunky 75 percent acrylic/25 percent wool bulky weight yarn (143 yds/100g per skein): 9 (10, 10, 11) skeins lime green #3335
- Size 10 (6mm) needles
- Size 11 (8mm) needles or size needed to obtain gauge
- Cable needle
- Stitch markers
- 7 (7, 8, 8) 1-inch buttons

GAUGE

18 sts and 19 rows = 4 inches/10cm in Cable pat with larger needles

14 sts and 19 rows = 4 inches/10cm in St st with larger needles

To save time, take time to check gauge.

BACK

With smaller needles, cast on 75 (83, 90, 98) sts.

Beg with purl row, work even in St st for 5 rows, changing to larger needles and inc 19 (21, 22, 24) sts evenly on last WS row. (94, 104, 112, 122 sts)

Referring to chart on page 45, beg and ending as indicated for chosen size, work even until back measures 13 (14, 14, 15) inches, ending with a WS row.

Shape armhole

Bind off 6 sts at beg of next 2 rows. (82, 92, 100, 110 sts)

Work even until armhole measures 8½ (8½, 9½, 9½) inches above bound-off underarm sts, ending with a WS row.

Shape neck

Work across 24 (29, 32, 37) sts; join 2nd ball of yarn and bind off next 34 (34, 36, 36) sts for back neck; work to end of row.

Working both sides of neck with separate balls of yarn, [dec 1 st at each neck edge] once. (23, 28, 31, 36 sts each side of neck)

Work even until armhole measures 9 (9, 10, 10) inches.

Bind off all shoulder sts.

LEFT FRONT

With smaller needles cast on 36 (40, 44, 48) sts.

Beg with purl row, work even in St st for 5 rows, changing to larger needle and inc 9 (10, 10, 11) sts evenly on last WS row. (45, 50, 54, 59 sts)

Referring to chart on page 45, beg as indicated for chosen size, work even until left front measures same as for back, ending with a WS row.

Shape armhole

Bind off 6 sts at beg of next row. (39, 44, 48, 53 sts)

Work even until armhole measures 7 (7, 8, 8) inches above bound-off underarm sts.

Shape neck

Continuing in established pat, bind off at neck edge 10 (10, 11, 11) sts once, 3 sts once, 2 sts once, 1 st once. (23, 28, 31, 36 sts each side of neck)

Work even until armhole measures same as for back.

Bind off shoulder sts.

RIGHT FRONT

With smaller needles cast on 36 (40, 44, 48) sts.

Beg with purl row, work even in St st for 5 rows, changing to larger needle and inc 9 (10, 10, 11) sts evenly on last WS row. (45, 50, 54, 59 sts)

Referring to chart, beg as indicated for chosen size, work even until right front measures same as for back, ending with a RS row.

Shape armhole
Bind off 6 sts at beg of next row. (39, 44, 48, 53 sts)

Work even until armhole measures 7 (7, 8, 8) inches above bound-off underarm sts.

Shape neck
Continuing in established pat, bind off at neck edge 10 (10, 11, 11) sts once, 3 sts once, 2 sts once, 1 st once. (23, 28, 31, 36 sts each side of neck)

Work even until armhole measures same as for back.

Bind off shoulder sts.

Sew shoulder seams.

COLLAR
With smaller needles and RS facing, beg at right front neck, pick up and knit 64 (64, 68, 68) sts evenly around neck.

Knit 5 rows, changing to larger needles on last row.

Work even in garter st until collar measures 3½ inches above picked up row.

Bind off loosely.

SLEEVE
With smaller needles, cast on 32 (32, 36, 36) sts.

Beg with purl row, work even in St st for 5 rows, changing to larger needle and inc 10 sts evenly on last WS row. (42, 42, 46, 46 sts)

Set up pat

Next row (RS): K0 (0, 2, 2) sts, pm, beg as indicated on chart, work next 42 sts cable pat, pm, k0 (0, 2, 2) sts.

Keeping sts between markers in established pat, and rem sts in St st, inc 1 st each end every 6th row 15 times, working added sts in St st. (72, 72, 76, 76 sts)

Work even until sleeve measures 20 (19, 18, 18) inches.

Bind off.

BUTTON BAND
With smaller needles pick up and knit 88 (92, 94, 100) sts evenly along left front edge.

Knit 5 rows.

Bind off.

BUTTONHOLE BAND

Pick up and knit as for button band.
Knit 1 row.

Buttonhole row (RS): K5 (3, 5, 4), [bind off 2 sts, k11(12, 10, 11) sts] 6 (6, 7, 7) times, bind off 2 sts, k3.

Next row: Knit, casting on 2 sts over each bound-off area.
Knit 2 rows.
Bind off.

ASSEMBLY

Sew sleeves into armholes.
Sew sleeve and side seams.
Sew on buttons opposite buttonholes. ■

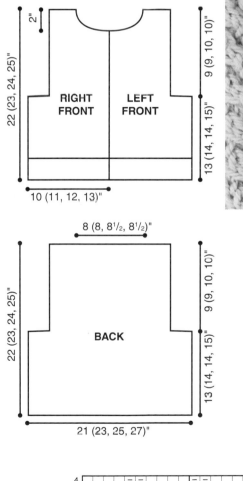

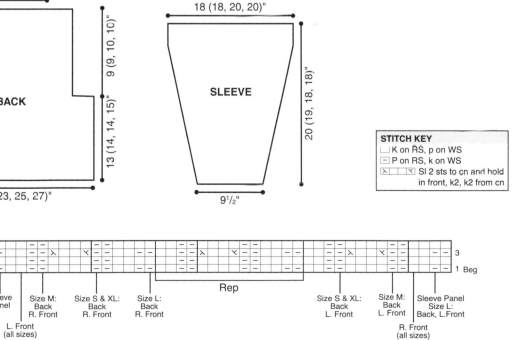

STITCH KEY
☐ K on RS, p on WS
⊟ P on RS, k on WS
⋋☐☐⋎ Sl 2 sts to cn and hold in front, k2, k2 from cn

Sleeve Panel

L. Front (all sizes)

Size M: Back R. Front

Size S & XL: Back R. Front

Size L: Back R. Front

Rep

Size S & XL: Back L. Front

Size M: Back L. Front

R. Front (all sizes)

Sleeve Panel Size L: Back, L.Front

MOM'S CASUAL CABLE CARDIGAN

KID'S CLASSIC CABLE PULLOVER

Design by Celeste Pinheiro

Rolled edges and cable patterning combine for a coordinating version of Mom's cardigan.

SIZE

Child's 2 (4, 6, 8) Instructions are given for smallest size, with larger sizes in parentheses. When only 1 number is given, it applies to all sizes.

SKILL LEVEL
■■■□
INTERMEDIATE

YARN WEIGHT
5
BULKY

FINISHED MEASUREMENTS

Chest: 26 (28, 30, 32) inches
Length: 15 (16, 17, 18) inches

MATERIALS

- Plymouth Encore Chunky 75 percent acrylic/25 percent wool bulky weight yarn (143 yds/100g per skein): 3 (4, 5, 5) skeins soft white #146
- Size 10 (6mm) straight and 16-inch needles
- Size 11 (8mm) needles or size needed to obtain gauge
- Cable needle
- Stitch markers

GAUGE

18 sts and 19 rows = 4 inches/10cm in Cable pat with larger needles

14 sts and 19 rows = 4 inches/10cm in St st with larger needles

To save time, take time to check gauge.

PATTERN NOTE

Cable pattern is very stretchy, take width measurement with piece in relaxed position.

BACK

With smaller needles cast on 46 (52, 56, 58 sts)

Beg with purl row, work even in St st for 5 rows, changing to larger needles and inc 12 (12, 12, 14) sts evenly on last WS row. (58, 64, 68, 72 sts)

Referring to chart on page 49, beg and ending as indicated for chosen size, work even in Cable pat

until back measures 9 (9½, 10½, 11) inches. Mark each end st for underarm.

Continue to work in established pat until back measures 14½ (15½, 15½, 17½) inches from beg, ending with a WS row.

Shape back neck

Work across 18 (20, 21, 22) sts; join 2nd ball of yarn and bind off next 22 (24, 26, 28) sts for back neck; work to end of row.

Work both sides of neck with separate balls of yarn, [dec 1 st at each neck edge] once. (17, 19, 20, 21 sts on each side of neck)

Work even until armhole measures 6 (6½, 6½, 7) inches above underarm marker. Bind off all shoulder sts.

FRONT

Work as for back until front measures 13 (14, 15, 16) inches from beg, ending with a WS row.

Shape neck

Work across 25 (28, 29, 31) sts; join 2nd ball of yarn and bind off next 8 (8, 10, 10) sts for front neck; work to end of row.

Work both sides of neck with separate balls of yarn, bind off at each neck edge [4 sts] 0 (0, 0, 1) time, [3 sts] once (twice, twice, once), [2 sts] twice (once, once, once), [1 st] once. (17, 19, 20, 21 sts each side of neck)

Work even until front measures same as for back above underarm marker.

Bind off all shoulder sts.
Sew shoulder seams.

NECK BAND

With RS facing and smaller circular needle, pick up and knit 22 (24, 26, 28) sts across back neck, 13 (14, 14, 15) sts along left neck edge, 8 (8, 10, 10) sts across front neck, and 13 (14, 14, 15) sts along right neck edge. (56, 60, 64, 68 sts)

Pm between first and last st.
Purl 1 rnd, knit 1 rnd, purl 1 rnd, knit 7 rnds.
Bind off loosely knitwise.

SLEEVES

With smaller needles cast on 30 (30, 32, 32) sts.

Beg with purl row, work even in St st for 5 rows, changing to larger needles and inc 6 sts evenly on last WS row. (36, 36, 38, 38 sts)

Set up pat

Next row (RS): K0 (0, 1, 1) st, pm, referring to chart, work Cable pat across next 36 sts, pm, k0 (0, 1, 1) st.

Keeping sts between markers in established Cable pat and rem sts in St st, [inc 1 st each end every 6th row] 4 (5, 4, 6) times, working added sts in St st. (44, 46, 46, 50 sts)

Work even until sleeve measures 10 (11, 12, 13) inches from beg.

Bind off all sts.

ASSEMBLY

Sew sleeves to body between underarm markers.

Sew sleeve and side seams. ■

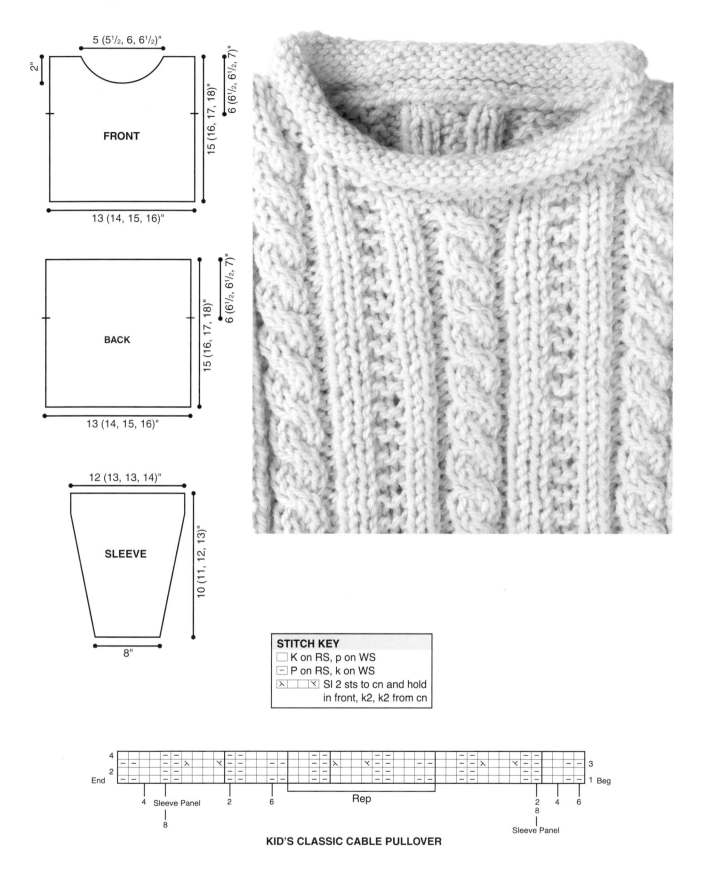

2"

5 (5½, 6, 6½)"

FRONT

15 (16, 17, 18)"

6 (6½, 6½, 7)"

13 (14, 15, 16)"

BACK

15 (16, 17, 18)"

6 (6½, 6½, 7)"

13 (14, 15, 16)"

12 (13, 13, 14)"

SLEEVE

10 (11, 12, 13)"

8"

STITCH KEY

☐ K on RS, p on WS

− P on RS, k on WS

⋋ ☐ ⋉ Sl 2 sts to cn and hold in front, k2, k2 from cn

4
2
End

Rep

4   Sleeve Panel   2   6

8

3
1 Beg

2   4   6
8
Sleeve Panel

KID'S CLASSIC CABLE PULLOVER

BRIGHT & CHEERY BABY SET

Design by Celeste Pinheiro

Baby will step out in style in a cabled and ribbed jacket with matching hat.

SIZE

Jacket: Infant's 6 month (12 month, 18 month, 24month) Instructions are given for smallest size, with larger sizes in parentheses. When only 1 number is given, it applies to all sizes.

Hat: One size only

SKILL LEVEL
INTERMEDIATE

YARN WEIGHT
5
BULKY

FINISHED MEASUREMENTS

Chest: 22 (24, 26, 28) inches
Length: 11 (12, 13, 14) inches
Hat circumference: Approx 16 inches

MATERIALS

- Plymouth Encore Chunky 75 percent acrylic/25 percent wool bulky weight yarn (143 yds/100g per skein): 4 (4, 5, 5) skeins hot pink #137
- Size 10 (6mm) needles
- Size 11 (8mm) needles or size needed to obtain gauge
- 4 (4, 5, 5) ¾-inch buttons
- Cable needle (cn)
- Stitch markers

GAUGE

18 sts and 19 rows = 4 inches/
10cm in Cable pat with larger
needles

14 sts and 19 rows = 4 inches/
10cm in St st with larger needles

To save time, take time to check
gauge.

Jacket

BACK

With smaller needles cast on 40
(44, 48, 52 sts)

Beg with purl row, work even
in St st for 5 rows, changing to
larger needles and inc 10 (10, 11,
12) sts evenly on last WS row. (50,
54, 58, 64 sts)

Referring to chart on page
53, beg and end as indicated for
chosen size, work even in cable
pat until back measures 6½ (7, 7½,
8) inches. Mark each end st for
underarm.

Continue to work in established
pat until back measures 11 (12, 13,
14) inches from beg.

Bind off all sts.

Mark center 20 (22, 24, 26) sts
for back neck.

LEFT FRONT

With smaller needles cast on 20
(22, 24, 26) sts.

Beg with purl row, work even in
St st for 5 rows, changing to larger
needles and inc 3 (3, 3, 4) sts
evenly on last WS row. (23, 25, 27,
30 sts)

Referring to chart, begin and
end as indicated for chosen size,
work even in cable pat until front
measures 6½ (7, 7½, 8) inches,
ending with a WS row.

Mark last st for underarm.

Continue to work in established
pat until front measures 3 (3½, 4,
4½) inches above underarm marker,
ending with a RS row.

Shape neck

Bind off at neck edge [3 (4, 5, 6)
sts] once, then [2 sts] twice.

[Dec 1 st at neck edge] once.
(15, 16, 17, 19 sts)

Work even until armhole
measures same as for back above
underarm marker.

RIGHT FRONT

With smaller needles cast on 20
(22, 24, 26) sts.

Beg with purl row, work even
in St st for 5 rows, changing to
larger needles and inc 3 (3, 3, 4)
sts evenly on last WS row. (23, 25,
27, 30 sts)

Referring to chart, begin and
end as indicated for chosen size,
work even in cable pat until front
measures 6½ (7, 7½, 8) inches,
ending with a WS row.

Mark last st for underarm.
Continue to work in established pat
until front measures 3 (3½, 4, 4½)
inches above underarm marker,
ending with a WS row.

Shape neck

Bind off at neck edge [3 (4, 5, 6)
sts] once, then [2 sts] twice.

[Dec 1 st at neck edge] once.
(15, 16, 17, 19 sts)

Work even until armhole
measures same as for back above
underarm marker.

Sew shoulder seams.

COLLAR

With smaller needles pick up and
knit 48 (52, 56, 60) sts evenly
around neck.

Knit 15 rows.
Bind off loosely.

BUTTON BAND

With smaller needles pick up and
knit 33 (37, 41, 45) sts evenly
along left edge.

Knit 3 rows.
Bind off.

BUTTONHOLE BAND

Pick up and knit as for button band.
Knit 1 row.

Buttonhole row (RS): K4 (5,
4, 4), [bind off 2 sts, k6 (7, 6, 7)
sts] 3 (3, 4, 4) times, bind off 2
sts, k3.

Knit 1 row, casting on 2 sts over
each bound-off area.

Bind off loosely.

SLEEVES

With smaller needles cast on 27
(27, 30, 32) sts.

Beg with purl row, work in St
st for 5 rows, changing to larger
needles on last WS row.

Continue in St st, [inc 1 st each
end every 6th row] 2 (4, 4, 5)
times. (31, 35, 38, 42 sts)

Work even until sleeve
measures 6½ (7, 8, 9) inches
from beg.

Bind off all sts.

ASSEMBLY

Sew sleeves to body between
underarm markers.

Sew sleeve and side seams.
Sew on buttons.

Hat

With smaller needles cast on
56 sts.

Beg with purl row, work in St
st for 5 rows, changing to larger
needles and inc 14 sts evenly on
last WS row. (70 sts)

Referring to chart, beg as
indicated and work 5 reps of Cable
pat until hat measures 3 inches
from beg, ending with a WS row.

Dec row (RS): Knit, dec 6 sts
evenly. (64 sts)

Purl 1 row.

Shape crown

Row 1 (RS): [K6, k2tog]
8 times. (56 sts)

Row 2 and all WS rows: Purl.

Row 3: [K5, k2tog] 8 times. (48 sts)

Row 5: [K4, k2tog] 8 times. (40 sts)

Continue to dec 8 sts every RS row in same manner until 8 sts rem.

Next row (WS): P2tog across. (4 sts)

I-CORD TRIM

*K4, sl sts back to LH needle; rep from * until cord measures 3 inches.

Next row: K4tog.

Cut yarn and pull through rem st.

ASSEMBLY

Sew seam.

Tie knot in I-cord. ■

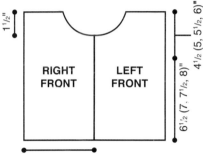

1½"

4½ (5, 5½, 6)"

6½ (7, 7½, 8)"

RIGHT FRONT LEFT FRONT

5 (5½, 6, 6½)"

4 (4½, 5, 5½)"

4½ (5, 5½, 6)"

6½ (7, 7½, 8)"

BACK

11 (12, 13, 14)"

9 (10, 11, 12)"

6½ (7, 8, 9)"

SLEEVE

6 (6, 6½, 7)"

STITCH KEY

☐ K on RS, p on WS

⊟ P on RS, k on WS

SI 2 sts to cn and hold in front, k2, k2 from cn

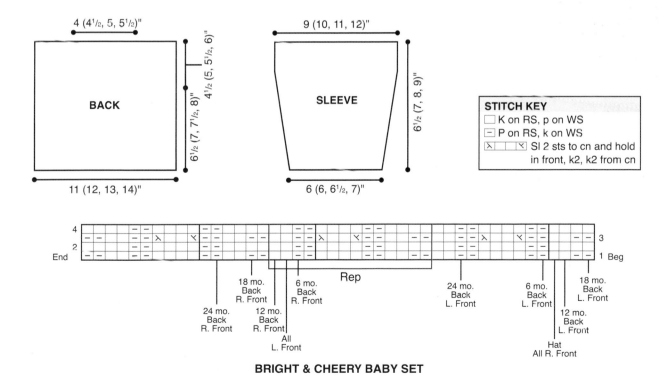

BRIGHT & CHEERY BABY SET

SNOWTIME CABLE SCARF

Design by Celeste Pinheiro

Ribs and cables combine in an easy pattern for a super-extended scarf.

SIZE
Adult

SKILL LEVEL
■■□□
EASY

YARN WEIGHT
(5)
BULKY

FINISHED MEASUREMENTS
Approx 7 x 70 inches, excluding fringe

MATERIALS
- Plymouth Encore Chunky 75 percent acrylic/25 percent wool (143 yds/100g per skein): 3 skeins blue #515
- Size 11 (8mm) needles or size needed to obtain gauge
- Cable needle
- Size J/10/6mm crochet hook

GAUGE
18 sts and 18 rows = 4 inches/ 10cm in cable pat.

To save time, take time to check gauge.

PATTERN STITCH
Cable & Rib
Row 1 (RS): *P2, k2, p2, k4, p2, k2; rep from * to last 2 sts, p2.
Row 2: P2 *p2, k2, p4, k2, p4; rep from * across.
Row 3: *P2, k2, p2, sl 2 sts to cn and hold in front, k2, k2 from cn, p2, k2; rep from * to last 2 sts, p2.
Row 4: Rep Row 2.

Rep Rows 1–4 for pat.

SCARF
Cast on 30 sts.

Beg with Row 2 of Cable & Rib pat, work even until scarf measures approx 70 inches, ending with Row 4.

Bind off in pat.

FRINGE
Cut 14-inch lengths of yarn. Referring to Fringe instructions on page 170, make Single Knot Fringe. Use 3 strands for each knot.

Tie knot in every 3rd st across cast-on and bound-off edges.

Trim fringe evenly. ■

DOG'S CABLE COMFORT SWEATER

Design by Celeste Pinheiro

Even Rover gets into the act with a chic pooch jacket.

SIZE
Small (medium) Instructions are given for smaller size, with larger size in parentheses. When only 1 number is given, it applies to both sizes.

SKILL LEVEL
INTERMEDIATE
YARN WEIGHT
5
BULKY

FINISHED MEASUREMENTS
Chest: 18 (22) inches
Length: 14 (18) inches

MATERIALS
- Plymouth Encore Chunky 75 percent acrylic/25 percent wool bulky weight yarn (143 yds/100g per skein): 2 (3) skeins turquoise #235
- Size 10 (6mm) needles
- Size 11 (8mm) needles or size needed to obtain gauge
- Cable needle
- Stitch holders
- 4 (5) ⅞-inch buttons

GAUGE
18 sts and 19 rows = 4 inches/ 10cm in cable pat with larger needles
To save time, take time to check gauge.

PATTERN NOTE
Sweater is knit from neck to tail.

SWEATER
With smaller needles, cast on 48 (62) sts.

Beg with purl row, work in St st for 5 rows, changing to larger needles on last WS row.

Set up pat
Next row (RS): K4, pm, referring to chart on page 56, work next 40 (54) sts in cable pat, pm, k4.

Keeping sts between markers in established pat, and 4 sts at each end in garter st, [inc 1 st each end every 4th row] 5 times, working added sts in garter st. (58, 72 sts)

Work even until piece measures 4 (5) inches from beg, ending with a WS row.

Beg leg openings
Next row (RS): K5, place rem sts on holder.

Work in garter st on these 5 sts only, until piece measures 6½ (8) inches from beg, ending with a WS row.

Do not cut yarn; place sts on holder.

Sl next 48 (62) sts to LH needle.

With RS facing, join yarn at leg opening.

Work even in established pat until piece measures 6½ (8) inches from beg, ending with a WS row.

Place sts on holder.

Sl rem 5 sts to LH needle.

With RS facing, join yarn at leg opening.

Work even in garter st until opening measures same as previous opening.

Next row (RS): Sl all sts to LH needle. Pick up dropped yarn of first section and work in pat across all sts.

Continue in established pat until piece measures 9 (12) inches from beg, ending with a WS row.

Shape tail section
Bind off 8 sts at beg of next 2 rows. (42, 56 sts)

[Dec 1 st each end every 4th row] 4 (5) times. (34, 46 sts)

Bind off.

BUTTON BAND
With smaller needles, pick up and knit 28 (40) sts evenly along left edge.

Knit 3 rows.

Bind off.

BUTTONHOLE BAND
With smaller needles, pick up and knit 28 (40) sts evenly along right edge.

Knit 1 row.

Buttonhole row (RS): K5, [bind off 2 sts, k4 (5)] 3 (4) times, bind off 2 sts, k3 (5).

Knit 1 row, casting on 2 sts over bound-off sts of previous row.

EDGING

With smaller needles and RS facing, pick up and knit 18 (20) sts along shaped tail section, 34 (46) sts across bound-off edge, and 18 (20) sts along remaining shaped tail section. (70, 86 sts)

Knit 3 rows.

Bind off loosely.

Sew on buttons. ■

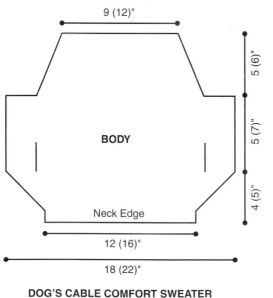

9 (12)"

5 (6)"

BODY

5 (7)"

4 (5)"

Neck Edge

12 (16)"

18 (22)"

DOG'S CABLE COMFORT SWEATER

STITCH KEY
☐ K on RS, p on WS
⊟ P on RS, k on WS
⋋⋌ Sl 2 sts to cn and hold in front, k2, k2 from cn

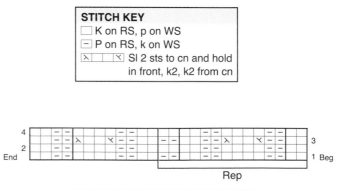

DOG'S CABLE COMFORT SWEATER

MOM'S SPECIAL OUTING CARDIGAN

Design by Kennita Tully

The occasion will be special when you take your daughter along and wear matching sweaters.

SIZE

Woman's small (medium, large, extra-large) Instructions are given for smallest size, with larger sizes in parentheses. When only 1 number is given, it applies to all sizes.

SKILL LEVEL
INTERMEDIATE

YARN WEIGHT
5
BULKY

FINISHED MEASUREMENTS

Chest: 37 (39, 41, 43) inches
Length: 19 (20, 21, 22) inches

MATERIALS

- Plymouth Baby Alpaca Grande 100 percent baby alpaca bulky weight yarn (110 yds/100g per skein): 7 (8, 9, 10) skeins plum #2213
- Size 11 (8mm) needles or size needed to obtain gauge
- Size J/10 (6mm) crochet hook
- 5 (5, 6, 6) ⅝-inch buttons

GAUGE

15 sts and 22 rows = 4 inches/ 10cm in Speckled Rib pat

12 sts and 16 rows = 4 inches/ 10cm in St st

To save time, take time to check gauge.

SPECIAL ABBRIEVATION

M1 (Make 1): Make a backward loop and place on RH needle.

PATTERN STITCH
Speckled Rib Pattern (multiple of 2 sts + 1)
Row 1 (RS): Knit.
Row 2: Purl.
Row 3: K1 *Sl 1p, K1; rep from * across.
Row 4: K1 *Sl 1p wyif, K1; rep from * across.
Row 5: Knit.
Row 6: Purl.
Row 7: K2, *sl 1p, k1; rep from * to last st, k1.
Row 8: K2, *sl 1p wyif, k1; rep from * to last st, k1.
Rep Rows 1–8 for pat.

PATTERN NOTES
Dec at neckline are worked on edge sts.

Inc for sleeves are worked using M1 and are worked one stitch in from edge.

BACK
Cast on 69 (73, 77, 81) sts.

Beg with Row 2 of Speckled Rib pat, work even until back measures 11 (11½, 12, 12½) inches, ending with a WS row.
Shape armhole
Bind off 10 sts at beg of next 2 rows. (49, 53, 57, 61 sts)

Work even until armhole measures 8 (8½, 9, 9½) inches above bound-off underarm sts. Bind off all sts.

Mark center 27 (29, 31, 33) sts for back neck.

RIGHT FRONT
Cast on 35 (37, 39, 41) sts.

Beg with Row 2 of Speckled Rib pat, work even until front measures same as for back to underarm, ending with a RS row.
Shape armhole
Bind off 10 sts at beg of next row. (25, 27, 29, 31 sts)

Work even until armhole measures 6 (6½, 7, 7½) inches

above bound-off underarm sts, ending with a WS row.
Shape neck
Bind off 7 (8, 9, 10) sts at beg of next row.

Dec 1 st at neck edge every other row 7 times. (11, 12, 13, 14 sts)

Work even until armhole measures same as for back above bound-off underarm sts.

Bind off.

LEFT FRONT
Cast on 35 (37, 39, 41) sts.

Beg with Row 2 of Speckled Rib pat, work even until front measures same as for back to underarm, ending with a WS row.
Shape armhole
Bind off 10 sts at beg of next row. (25, 27, 29, 31 sts)

Work even until armhole

measures 6 (6½, 7, 7½) inches above bound-off underarm sts, ending with a RS row.
Shape neck
Bind off 7 (8, 9, 10) sts at beg of next row.

Dec 1 st at neck edge every other row 7 times. (11, 12, 13, 14 sts)

Work even until armhole measures same as for back above bound-off underarm sts.

Bind off.

SLEEVES
Cast on 27 (29, 31, 33) sts.

Working in St st, inc 1 st each end of 5th row, then [every 6 rows] 5 (4, 3, 2) times, and [every 8 rows] 5 (6, 7, 8) times. (49, 51, 53, 55 sts)

Work even until sleeve measures 18 (19½, 19½, 20) inches.

Mark each end st for underarm.

Work even for 2½ (2½, 3, 3) inches more.

Bind off.

EDGING

Note: *If not familiar with single crochet st, refer to page 173.*

With crochet hook, work 1 row sc across lower edge of sleeve. Do not turn.

Working from left to right, work1sc in each sc of previus row. Fasten off.

ASSEMBLY

Sew shoulder seams.

Sew sleeves into armholes, matching underarm markers to first bound-off st of body.

Sew sleeve and side seams.

BODY EDGING

Beg at side seam with crochet hook, work 1 row sc across around entire lower, front and neck edges. Join with sl st. Do not turn.

Mark right front edge for 5 (5, 6, 6) buttons evenly spaced.

Working from left to right, work 1sc in each sc of previous row, skipping a sc at each of previous row, skipping marker to form buttonhole.

Fasten off.

Sew on buttons. ■

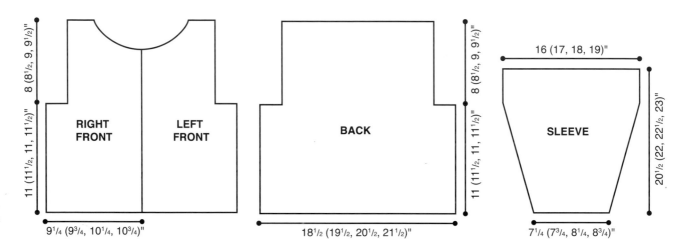

DAUGHTER'S SPECIAL OUTING CARDIGAN

Design by Kennita Tully

Any little girl will love to tag along with Mom in her matching cardigan.

SIZE

Girl's 4 (6, 8, 10)
Instructions are given
for smallest size,
with larger sizes in
parentheses. When
only 1 number is given, it applies to
all sizes.

FINISHED MEASUREMENTS

Chest: 26 (28, 30, 32) inches
Length: 14 (15, 16, 17) inches

MATERIALS

- Plymouth Baby Alpaca Grande 100 percent baby alpaca bulky weight yarn (110 yds/100g per skein): 4 (5, 6, 7) balls sea foam blue #3317
- Size 11 (8mm) needles or size needed to obtain gauge
- Size J/10/6mm crochet hook
- 4 (4, 5, 5) ⅝-inch buttons

GAUGE

15 sts and 22 rows = 4 inches/
10cm in Speckled Rib pat
    12 sts and 16 rows = 4 inches/
10cm in St st
    To save time, take time to check gauge.

SPECIAL ABBREVIATION

M1 (Make 1): Make a backward loop and place on RH needle.

PATTERN STITCH

Speckled Rib (multiple of 2 sts + 1)
Row 1 (RS): Knit.
Row 2: Purl.
Row 3: K1, *sl 1p, k1; rep from * across.
Row 4: K1, *sl 1p wyif, k1; rep from * across.
Row 5: Knit.
Row 6: Purl.
Row 7: K2, *sl 1p, k1; rep from * to last st, k1.
Row 8: K2, *sl 1p wyif, k1; rep from * to last st, k1.
Rep Rows 1–8 for pat.

PATTERN NOTES

Dec at neckline are worked on edge sts.
    Incs for sleeves are worked using M1 and are worked 1 stitch in from edge.

BACK

Cast on 49 (53, 57, 61) sts.
    Beg with Row 2 of Speckled Rib pat, work even until back measures 8 (8½, 9, 9½) inches, ending with a WS row.

Shape armhole

Bind off 6 (6, 8, 8) sts at beg of next 2 rows. (37, 41, 41, 45 sts)
    Work even until armhole measures 6 (6½, 7, 7½) inches above bound-off underarm sts.

Bind off all sts.
    Mark center 17 (19, 21, 23) sts for back neck.

RIGHT FRONT

Cast on 25 (27, 29, 31) sts.
    Beg with Row 2 of Speckled Rib pat, work even until front measures same as for back to underarm, ending with a RS row.

Shape armhole

Bind off 6 (6, 8, 8) sts at beg of next row. (19, 21, 21, 23 sts)
    Work even until armhole measures 4 (4½, 5, 5½) inches above bound-off underarm sts, ending with a WS row.

Shape neck

Bind off 4 (5, 6, 7) sts at beg of next row.
    Dec 1 st at neck edge every other row 5 times. (10, 11, 10, 11 sts)
    Work even until armhole measures same as for back above bound-off underarm sts.
    Bind off.

LEFT FRONT

Cast on 25 (27, 29, 31) sts.
    Beg with Row 2 of Speckled Rib pat, work even until front measures same as for back to underarm, ending with a WS row.

Shape armhole

Bind off 6 (6, 8, 8) sts at beg of next row. (19, 21, 21, 23 sts)

Work even until armhole measures 4 (4½, 5, 5½) inches above bound-off underarm sts, ending with a RS row.

Shape neck

Bind off 4 (5, 6, 7) sts at beg of next row.

Dec 1 st at neck edge every other row 5 times. (10, 11, 10, 11 sts)

Work even until armhole measures same as for back above bound-off underarm sts.

Bind off.

SLEEVES

Cast on 19 (21, 23, 25) sts.

Working in St st, inc 1 st each end on 3rd (5th, 5th, 5th) row, then [every 6 rows] 8 (8, 7, 6) times, and [every 0 (0, 8, 8) rows] 0 (0, 1, 2) times. (37, 39, 41, 43 sts)

Work even until sleeve measures 13 (13½, 13½, 14) inches.

Mark each end st for underarm.

Work even for 2 (2, 2½, 2½) inches more.

Bind off.

SLEEVE EDGING

Note: *If not familiar with single crochet st, refer to page 173-174.*

With crochet hook, work 1 row sc across lower edge of sleeve. Do not turn.

Working from left to right, work 1 reverse sc in each sc of previous row.

Fasten off.

ASSEMBLY

Sew shoulder seams.

Sew sleeves into armholes, matching underarm markers to first bound-off st of body.

Sew sleeve and side seams

BODY EDGING

Beg at side seam with crochet hook, work 1 row sc around entire lower, front and neck edges. Join with sl st.

Do not turn.

Mark right front edge for 4 (4, 5, 5) evenly spaced buttonholes.

Working in the opposite direction, work reverse 1sc in each sc in previous row, skipping sc at each marker to form buttonhole.

Fasten off.

Sew on buttons ■

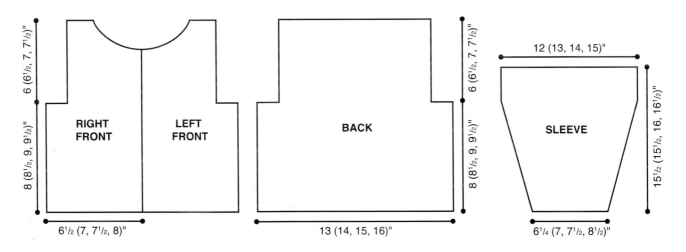

FIRST CLASS LEISURE PULLOVER

Design by Katharine Hunt

The comfortable ribbed pattern of this attractive crew neck pullover will appeal to men.

SIZE

Man's medium (large, extra-large, 2X-large) Instructions are given for smallest size, with larger sizes in parentheses. When only 1 number is given, it applies to all sizes.

SKILL LEVEL
INTERMEDIATE

YARN WEIGHT
5
BULKY

A

SKILL LEVEL
INTERMEDIATE

YARN WEIGHT
4
MEDIUM

B

FINISHED MEASUREMENTS

Chest: 42½ (47½, 52½, 57) inches
Length: 25½ (26½, 27, 27½) inches

MATERIALS

- Plymouth Encore Chunky 75 percent acrylic/25 percent wool bulky weight yarn (143 yds/100g per skein): 8 (9, 10, 11) skeins blue/green heather #670 (A)
- Plymouth LeFibre Nobili Imperiale Print 80 percent super kid mohair/20 percent nylon worsted weight yarn (109 yds/25g per ball): 11 (12, 13, 15) balls green print #4183 (B)
- Size 10½ (6.5mm) straight and 16-inch circular needles
- Size 11 (8mm) straight needles or size needed to obtain gauge
- Stitch markers

GAUGE

13 sts and 17 rows = 4 inches/
10cm in Ribs pat with larger
needles, lightly blocked

To save time, take time to
check gauge.

SPECIAL ABBREVIATION

M1 (Make 1): Knit or purl
(as pat dictates) into the front and
back of st.

PATTERN STITCHES

A. 1/1 Rib

Row 1 (RS): K1, *p1, k1; rep from
* across.
Row 2: P1, *k1, p1; rep from *
across.
Rep Rows 1 and 2 for pat.

B. Seeded Rib (multiple of 4 sts + 1)
Row 1 (RS): P1, *k3, p1; rep from
* across.
Row 2: K2, p1, *k3, p1; rep from *
to last 2 sts, k2.
Rep Rows 1 and 2 for pat.

PATTERN NOTE

Two strands of yarn (one each of
A and B) are held tog for
entire garment.

BACK

With smaller needles and 1 strand
each of A and B held tog, cast on
69 (77, 85, 93) sts.

Work even in 1/1 Rib pat for 2
(2, 2½, 2½) inches, ending with a
WS row.

Change to larger needles and
work even in Seeded Rib pat until
back measures 15½ (16, 16½, 16½)
inches, ending with a WS row.

Shape armholes

Bind off 7 (9, 11, 11) sts at beg of
next 2 rows.

[Dec 1 st each end every other
row] 3 (3, 3, 5) times. (49, 53, 57,
61 sts)

Work even until armhole
measures 10 (10½, 10½, 11)

inches above bound-off underarm
sts, ending with a WS row.

Shape shoulders and back neck

Work across 15 (17, 18, 19) sts;
join 2nd ball of each yarn and bind
off next 19 (19, 21, 23) sts for back
neck; work across rem 15 (17, 18,
19) sts.

Work both sides of neck at
same time with separate balls of
yarn, [dec 1 st at each neck edge]
twice, *at the same time* bind off at
each arm edge 6 (7, 8, 8) sts once,
then 7 (8, 8, 9) sts once.

FRONT

Work as for back until armhole
measures 8 inches above bound-
off underarm sts, ending with a
WS row.

Shape front neck

Next row (RS): Work across 18
(20, 21, 23) sts; join 2nd ball of
each yarn and bind off next 13 (13,
15, 15) sts; work across rem 18
(20, 21, 23) sts.

Work both sides of neck with
separate balls of yarn, [dec 1 st at

each neck edge every other row] 5
(5, 5, 6) times. (13, 15, 16, 17 sts
each side of neck)

Work even until armholes
measure same as back, ending with
a WS row.

Shape shoulders

Bind off at each arm edge 6 (7,
8, 8) sts once, then 7 (8, 8, 9)
sts once.

SLEEVES

With smaller needles and 1 strand
each of A and B held tog, cast on
33 (35, 35, 37) sts.

Work even in 1/1 Rib pat for 2
(2, 2½, 2½) inches, ending with a
WS row.

Change to larger needles and
work even in Seeded Rib pat for
2 rows.

Inc 1 st each end on next, then
every following 4th row 16 (16, 17,
17) times, working added sts into
pat. (65, 67, 69, 71 sts)

Work even until sleeve
measures 18 (18½, 19, 19) inches
or desired length.

Mark each end st for underarm.

Shape sleeve cap

Work even for 2½ (3, 3½, 3½) inches more, ending with a WS row.

[Dec 1 st each end every other row] 5 times.

Bind off rem 55 (57, 59, 61) sts.

ASSEMBLY

Sew shoulder seams.

NECK BAND

Beg at left shoulder seam with smaller circular needle, pick up and knit 12 (13, 13, 15) sts along left neck edge, 15 (15, 17, 17) sts across front neck, 12 (13, 13, 15) sts along right neck edge, and 31 (31, 33, 35) sts across back neck. (70, 72, 76, 82 sts)

Place marker between first and last st.

Next 6 rnds: *K1, p1; rep from * around.

Bind off in rib.

FINISHING

Sew sleeves into armhole, matching underarm markers to first bound-off underarm st on body.

Sew sleeve and side seams. ■

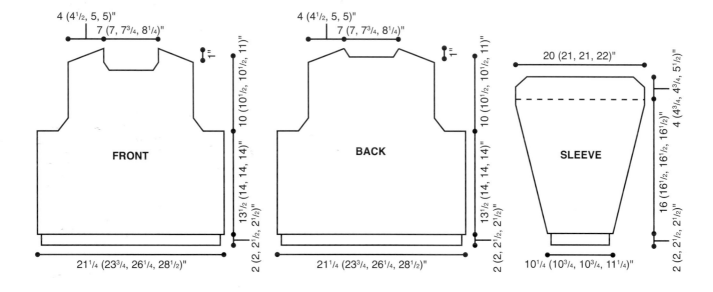

FRONT

4 (4½, 5, 5)"

7 (7, 7¾, 8¼)"

1"

10 (10½, 10½, 11)"

13½ (14, 14, 14)"

2 (2, 2½, 2½)"

21¼ (23¾, 26¼, 28½)"

BACK

4 (4½, 5, 5)"

7 (7, 7¾, 8¼)"

1"

10 (10½, 10½, 11)"

13½ (14, 14, 14)"

2 (2, 2½, 2½)"

21¼ (23¾, 26¼, 28½)"

SLEEVE

20 (21, 21, 22)"

4 (4¾, 4¾, 5½)"

16 (16½, 16½, 16½)"

2 (2, 2½, 2½)"

10¼ (10¾, 10¾, 11¼)"

CHECK-IN FOR FUN HOODIE PULLOVER

Design by Katharine Hunt

Two earthy shades are used in a short outdoor pullover with a hood and zip front.

SIZE
Woman's small (medium, large) Instructions are given for smallest size, with larger sizes in parentheses. When only 1 number is given, it applies to all sizes.

SKILL LEVEL
INTERMEDIATE

YARN WEIGHT
4
MEDIUM

FINISHED MEASUREMENTS
Chest: 38 (42, 46) inches
Length: 22 (23, 24) inches

MATERIALS
- Plymouth Encore Worsted 75 percent acrylic/25 percent wool worsted weight yarn (200 yds/ 100g per skein): 7 (8, 9) skeins beige heather #1415 (MC)
- Plymouth Encore Colorspun Worsted 75 percent acrylic/25 percent wool worsted weight yarn (200 yds/100g per skein): 4 (4, 5) skeins tweed #7172 (CC)
- Size 6 (4mm) 24-inch circular needle
- Size 10½ (6.5mm) needles
- Size 11 (8mm) needles or size needed to obtain gauge
- Stitch holder
- Size H/8/5mm crochet hook
- 6-inch zipper

GAUGE

15 sts and 25 rows = 4 inches/ 10cm in Block pat with size 11 needles, lightly blocked

To save time, take time to check gauge.

SPECIAL ABBREVIATIONS

M1 (Make 1): Knit or purl into front and back of st as side of work dictates.

Cable Cast-On: *Insert RH needle between last 2 sts of LH needle, wrap yarn around RH needle as if to knit and pull yarn through to make a new st, place new st on LH needle; rep from * as directed.

PATTERN STITCH
Block

Rows 1 (RS) and 2: With A, Knit.
Row 3: With B, k1, *sl 2 wyib, k2; rep from * to last 3 sts, sl 2 wyib, k1.
Row 4: With B, p1, *sl 2 wyif, p2; rep from * to last 3 sts, sl 2 wyif, p1.

Rep Rows 1–4 for pat.

PATTERN NOTE

Two strands of yarn are held tog for entire garment.

BACK

With size 10½ needles and MC, cast on 72 (80, 88) sts.
Row 1 (RS): P1, *k2, p2; rep from * to last 3 sts, k2, p1.
Row 2: K1, *p2, k2; rep from * to last 3 sts, p2, k1.

Change to size 11 needles and work even in Block pat until back measures 12½ (13, 13½) inches, ending with a WS row.

Shape armholes

Bind off 12 sts at beg of next 2 rows. (48, 56, 64 sts)

Work even until armhole measures 8½ (9, 9½) inches, ending with a WS row.

Shape shoulders and back neck

Mark center 16 (18, 20) sts.

Work to marker; join 2nd double strand of yarn and bind off marked sts; work to end of row. (16, 19, 22 sts on each side of neck)

Work both sides of neck with separate balls of yarn, [dec 1 st each side of neck every row] twice, *at the same time* bind off at each arm edge 4 (4, 5) sts twice, then 0 (4, 5) sts once, and finally 6 (5, 5) sts once.

FRONT

Work as for back until front measures 2¼ inches above bound-off underarm sts, ending with a WS row.

Divide for neck opening

Work across 24 (28, 32) sts; place rem sts on holder.

Beg left side

Work even on left front until armhole measures 6 (6½, 7) inches above bound-off underarm sts, ending with a RS row.

Shape front neck

Bind off 5 (6, 7) sts, work to end of row. (19, 22, 25 sts)

[Dec 1 st at neck edge every row] 3 times, then [every other row] twice. (14, 17, 20 sts)

Work even until armhole measures same as for back above bound-off underarm sts, ending with a WS row.

Shape shoulder

Bind off at arm edge 4 (4, 5) sts twice, then 0 (4, 5) sts once, and finally 6 (5, 5) sts once.

Beg right side

Sl sts from holder to needle.

Work even on right front until armhole measures 6 (6½, 7) inches above bound-off underarm sts, ending with a WS row.

Shape front neck

Bind off 5 (6, 7) sts, work to end of row. (19, 22, 25 sts)

[Dec 1 st at neck edge every row] 3 times, then [every other row] twice. (14, 17, 20 sts)

Work even until armhole measures same as for back above

bound-off underarm sts, ending with a RS row.

Shape shoulder

Bind off at arm edge 4 (4, 5) sts twice, then 0 (4, 5) sts once, and finally 6 (5, 5) sts once.

SLEEVES

With size 10½ needles and MC, cast on 32 (34, 36) sts.

Work 2 rows of ribbing as for back.

Change to size 11 needles and work Rows 1 and 2 of Block pat.

Size medium only: Beg and end Row 3 of pat with k2 instead of k1, and Row 4 with p2 instead of p1.

Working in established pat, inc 1 st each end of Row 5 and [every following 4th row] 3 (4, 4) times, then [every 6th row] 12 (12, 13) times. (64, 68, 72 sts)

Work even until sleeve measures 16½ (17, 17½) inches from beg.

Mark each end st of last row for underarm.

Work even for approx 3¼ inches more, ending with Row 4 of Block pat.

Change to size 10½ needles. Knit 1 row.

Bind off knitwise on WS.

HOOD
Left Half

With size 10½ needles and MC, cast on 2 sts.

Row 1 (RS): K1, M1. (3 sts)
Row 2: M1, p2. (4 sts)
Row 3: K3, M1. (5 sts)

Work in St st, [inc 1 st at neck edge every row as established] 7 (7, 9) times more. (12, 12, 14 sts)

Next row: Using Cable cast-on method, cast on 17 (18, 19) sts. (29, 30, 33 sts)

Work even for 3 rows.

Inc 1 st at same edge on next and every following 4th row twice. (32, 33, 36 sts)

Work even for 6 (6, 6½) inches, ending with WS row.

Shape top

Dec row (RS): Ssk, knit to end of row.

Next row: Purl.

Rep these 2 rows 5 times more; then rep Dec row only 4 (4, 5) times. (22, 23, 25 sts)

[Dec 1 st each end every row] 3 times. (16, 17, 19 sts)

Bind off rem sts.

Right Half

With size 10½ needles and MC, cast on 2 sts.

Row 1 (RS): K1, M1. (3 sts)

Row 2: P2, M1. (4 sts)

Row 3: M1, k3. (5 sts)

Work in St st, [inc 1 st at neck edge every row as established] 7 (7, 9) times more. (12, 12, 14 sts)

Next row: Using Cable cast-on method, cast on 17 (18, 19) sts. (29, 30, 33 sts)

Work even for 3 rows.

Inc 1 st at same edge on next and every following 4th row twice. (32, 33, 36 sts)

Work even for 6 (6, 6½) inches, ending with WS row.

Shape top

Dec row (RS): Knit to last 2 sts, k2tog.

Next row: Purl.

Rep these 2 rows 5 times more; then rep Dec row only 4 (4, 5) times. (22, 23, 25 sts)

[Dec 1 st each end every row] 3 times. (16, 17, 19 sts) Bind off rem sts.

Sew hood pieces tog along shaped back and top seam.

HOOD BAND

With RS facing and size 6 circular needle, pick up and knit 100 (100, 104) sts along front edge of hood.

Row 1 (WS): P1, *k2, p2; rep from * to last 3 sts, k2, p1.

Row 2: K1, *p2, k2; rep from * to last 3 sts, p2, k1.

Bind off in pat.

ASSEMBLY

Note: *If not familiar with single crochet st, refer to page 173.*

With crochet hook and MC, work 1 row of sc around front opening.

Sew zipper into front opening, having front edges meet to conceal zipper teeth.

Sew shoulder seams.

Sew hood to body, easing around neck shaping.

Sew sleeves into armholes, matching underarm markers to first bound-off underarm st of body.

Sew sleeve and side seams. ■

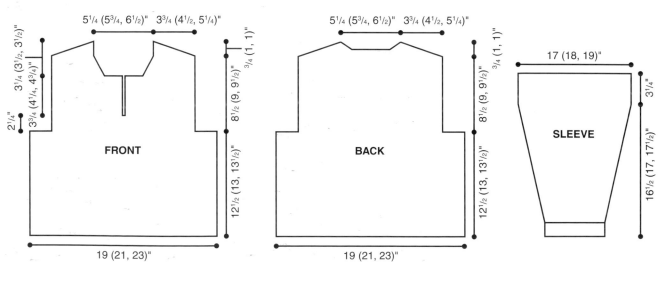

FUN & FURRY SWEATER JACKET

Design by Barbara Venishnick

This fine feathered jacket is dressy enough for an evening out and wild enough to wear over jeans.

SIZE

Woman's small (medium, large, extra-large) Instructions are given for smallest size, with larger sizes in parentheses. When only 1 number is given, it applies to all sizes

SKILL LEVEL
INTERMEDIATE

YARN WEIGHT
6 SUPER BULKY

MC

SKILL LEVEL
INTERMEDIATE

YARN WEIGHT
4 MEDIUM

CC

FINISHED MEASUREMENTS

Chest (closed): 38 (43, 46, 50) inches

Length: 23 (23½, 24, 24½) inches

MATERIALS

• Plymouth Parrot 100 percent nylon super bulky novelty ribbon yarn (28 yds/50g per ball): 14 (15, 16, 17) balls blue/purple variegated #6 (MC)

• Plymouth Fantasy Naturale 100 percent mercerized cotton worsted weight yarn (100g/140 yds per skein): 2 (3, 3, 3) skeins dark pink #8016 (CC)

• Size 7 (4.5mm) straight and 16-inch circular needles

• Size 15 (10mm) needles or size needed to obtain gauge

• 20-inch separating zipper

• Stitch holders

GAUGE

8½ sts and 14 rows = 4 inches/ 10cm in rev St st with larger needles

To save time, take time to check gauge.

SPECIAL ABBREVIATION

Cable Cast-On: *Insert RH needle between last 2 sts of LH needle, wrap yarn around RH needle as if to knit and pull yarn through to make a new st, place new st on LH needle; rep from * as directed.

PATTERN STITCH

2/2 Rib

Row 1 (RS): K2, *p2, k2; rep from * across.

Row 2: P2, *k2, p2; rep from * across.

Rep Rows 1 and 2 for pat.

PATTERN NOTE

It is best to work both fronts at same time as well as both sleeves at the same time because MC is so heavily textured it is difficult to count rows after knitting is complete. This will ensure that both fronts and both sleeves are the same length.

BACK

With smaller needles and CC, cast on 82 (90, 98, 106) sts.

Work even in 2/2 Rib for 3 inches, ending with a WS row.

Change to MC and larger needles.

Dec row (RS): K2tog across. (41, 45, 49, 53 sts)

Work even in rev St st until back measures 13 inches.

Shape underarms

Bind off 2 (2, 3, 3) sts at beg of next 2 rows, 1 (2, 2, 2) sts at beg of following 2 rows, then 1 (1, 1, 2) sts at the beg of next 2 rows.

Next row: Dec 1 st each end. (31, 33, 35, 37 sts)

Work even until armhole measures 9 (9½, 10, 10½) inches

above first set of bound-off underarm sts.

Shape shoulders

Bind off at each arm edge 3 (3, 4, 4) sts twice, then 3 (4, 3, 4) sts once.

Bind off rem 13 sts for back neck.

LEFT FRONT

With smaller needles and CC, cast on 41 (45, 49, 53) sts.

Ending with k1 on RS rows and beg with p1 on WS rows, work even in 2/2 rib for 3 inches ending with a WS row.

Change to MC and larger needles.

Dec row (RS): K2tog to last st, k1. (21, 23, 25, 27 sts)

Work even in rev St st until front measures same as back to underarm.

Shape underarm

Bind off at arm edge, 2 (2, 3, 3) sts once, 1 (2, 2, 2) sts once, then 1 (1, 1, 2) sts once.

Next row: Dec 1 st at arm edge. (16, 17, 18, 19 sts)

Work even until armhole measures 7 inches above first set of bound-off underarm sts, ending with a RS row.

Shape neck

Next row (WS): Bind off 5 sts, knit to end of row.

[Dec 1 st at neck edge every RS row] twice.

Work even on rem 9 (10, 11, 12) sts until armhole measures same as for back.

Shape shoulder

Bind off at arm edge 3 (3, 4, 4) sts twice, then 3 (4, 3, 4) sts once.

RIGHT FRONT

With smaller needles and CC, cast on 41 (45, 49, 53) sts.

Beg with k1 on RS rows and end with p1 on WS rows, work even in 2/2 rib for 3 inches ending with a WS row.

Change to MC and larger needles.

Dec row (RS): K1, *k2tog; rep from * across. (21, 23, 25, 27 sts)

Work even in rev St st until front measures same as back to underarm.

Shape underarm

Bind off at arm edge, 2 (2, 3, 3) sts once, 1 (2, 2, 2) sts once, then 1 (1, 1, 2) sts once.

Next row: Dec 1 st at arm edge. (16, 17, 18, 19 sts)

Work even until armhole measures 7 inches above first set of bound-off underarm sts, ending with a WS row.

Shape neck

Next row (RS): Bind off 5 sts, knit to end of row.

[Dec 1 st at neck edge every RS row] twice.

Work even on rem 9 (10, 11, 12) sts until armhole measures same as for back.

Shape shoulder

Bind off at arm edge 3 (3, 4, 4) sts twice, then 3 (4, 3, 4) sts once.

SLEEVES

With smaller needles and CC, cast on 42 sts.

Work even in 2/2 Rib for 3 inches, ending with a WS row.

Change to MC and larger needles.

Dec row (RS): *K2, [k2tog] twice; rep from * across. (28 sts)

Working in rev St st, [inc 1 st each end every 4th row] 4 (5, 6, 7) times. (36, 38, 40, 42 sts)

Work even until sleeve measures 17 inches, ending with a WS row.

Shape sleeve cap

Bind off 2 (2, 3, 3) sts at beg of next 2 rows, 1 (2, 2, 2) sts at beg of following 2 rows, then 1 (1, 1, 2) sts at the beg of next 2 rows.

[Dec 1 st each end every other row] 6 times. (16 sts)

Bind off 2 sts at beg of next 4 rows.

Bind off rem 8 sts.

Sew sleeves into armholes matching underarm shaping.
Sew sleeve and side seams.

COLLAR

With RS facing using smaller circular needle and CC, (k1, p2, k2) from right front band holder, turn, Cable cast on 66 (66, 70, 70) sts, turn, (k2, p2, k1) from left front band holder. (76, 76, 80,80 sts)

Next row: P1, work in established 2/2 Rib to last st, p1.

Work even in established pat until collar measures 4½ inches above cast-on edge.

Bind off loosely in pat.

Sew cast-on edge of collar to neckline.

MOCK POCKET FLAPS
Make 2

With smaller needles and CC, cast on 18 sts.

Work even in 2/2 Rib for 8 rows.

Shape end

Bind off 3 sts at beg of next 5 rows.

Bind off rem 3 sts.

Referring to photo, pin mock pocket flaps to fronts of jacket.

Sew in place along cast-on edge, stretching slightly. ■

RIGHT FRONT BAND

With smaller needles and CC, cast on 5 sts.

Row 1 (WS): P2, k2, p1.

Row 2: K1, p2, k2.

Rep these 2 rows until band measures 20 inches.

Place sts on holder.

LEFT FRONT BAND

With smaller needles and CC, cast on 5 sts.

Row 1 (WS): P1, k2, p2.

Row 2: K2, p2, k1.

Rep these 2 rows until band measures 20 inches.

Place sts on holder.

ASSEMBLY

Pin, then sew left and right bands to corresponding sides of zipper.

Pin, then sew zipper assembly to corresponding fronts of jacket.

Sew shoulder seams.

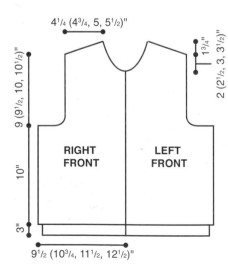

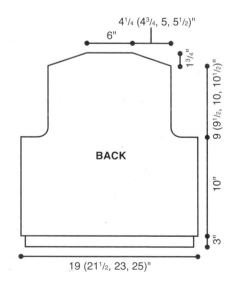

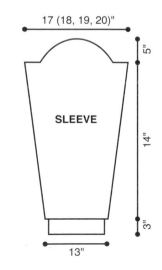

SKY'S THE LIMIT JACKET

Design by Pauline Schultz

This double-bottoned jacket is just the thing that will keep you warm and in style.

SIZE

Woman's small (medium, large) Instructions are given for smallest size, with larger sizes in parentheses. When only 1 number is given, it applies to all sizes.

FINISHED MEASUREMENTS

Chest: 38 (42, 48, 52) inches
Length: 19 (19½, 20, 20½) inches

MATERIALS

- Plymouth Yukon Print 35 percent mohair/35 percent wool, 30 percent acrylic super bulky weight yarn (59 yds/100g per skein): 9 (11, 13, 14) skeins blue haze #2004
- Size 15 (10mm) 29-inch circular needle or size needed to obtain gauge
- Stitch markers
- Stitch holders
- Matching lighter weight yarn for sewing seams

GAUGE

10½ sts and 15 rows = 4 inches/ 10cm in Ladder pat
   To save time, take time to check gauge.

SPECIAL ABBREVIATIONS

Cable Cast-On: *Insert RH needle between last 2 sts of LH needle, wrap yarn around RH needle as if to knit and pull yarn through to make a new st, place new st on LH needle; rep from * as directed.

M1 (Make 1): Make a backward loop and place on RH needle.

PATTERN STITCHES

Seed Stitch

Row 1: *K1, p1; rep from * across.

Row 2: Purl the knit sts and knit the purl sts as they present themselves.

Rep Row 2 for pat.

Ladder Stitch

Row 1 (RS): *P2, k6 (7, 7, 6); rep from * to last 2 sts, p2.

Row 2: Knit or purl the sts as they present themselves.

Rows 3 and 4: Rep Rows 1 and 2.

Row 5: *P10 (11, 11, 10), k6 (7, 7, 6); rep from * to last 10 (11, 11, 10) sts, p10 (11, 11, 10).

Row 6: *K2, p6 (7, 7, 6); rep from * to last 2 sts, k2.

Rows 7–10: Rep Rows 1–4.

Row 11: P2, *k6 (7, 7, 6), p10 (11, 11, 10); rep from * to last 8 (9, 9, 8) sts, k6 (7, 7, 6), p2.

Row 12: *K2, p6 (7, 7, 6); rep from * to last 2 sts, p2.

Rep Rows 1–12 for pat.

PATTERN NOTES

St counts include all selvage sts.

Work dec as follows:

RS knit dec: K2tog, work in pat to last 2 sts, k2tog-tbl.

RS purl dec: P2tog, work in pat to last 2 sts, p2tog-tbl.

WS knit dec: K2tog, work in pat to last 2 sts, skp.

WS purl dec: P2tog-tbl, work in pat to last 2 sts, p2tog-tbl.

BODY

Cast on 110 (121, 139, 142) sts

using cable cast-on technique.

Set up pat (WS): [P1-tbl, k1-tbl] 5 times, place marker, [k2-tbl, p6 (7, 7, 6)-tbl] 11(11, 13, 15) times, k2-tbl, pm, [p1-tbl, k1-tbl] 5 times.

Keeping 10 sts at each end in Seed pat, and sts between markers in Ladder pat, work even for 4 rows.

*Buttonhole row (RS): K1, p1, k1, yo, k2tog, p1, k1, yo, k2tog, p1, work in pat to end of row.

Work 11 rows even*; rep from * to * once. Work Buttonhole row.

Work even until body measures 10 (10½, 10½, 11) inches from beg, ending with a WS row.

Divide for fronts and back

Next row (RS): Work across 28 (30, 33, 34) sts and place on holder for right front, bind off next 6 (7, 10, 10) sts for right underarm, work across 42 (47, 53, 54) sts and place on 2nd holder for back, bind off next 6 (7, 10, 10) sts for left underarm, work to end of row.

LEFT FRONT

Shape underarm and neck

Work even for 1 row.

Keeping 1 st at arm edge in St st, [dec 1 st at arm edge every row] 3 (4, 5, 5) times, *at the same time* dec 1 st before marker on this and every following 4th row 7 (7, 7, 8) times. (18, 19, 21, 21 sts)

Work even in pat until armhole measures 8½ (8½, 9, 9) inches above bound-off underarm sts, ending with a WS row.

Bind off 7 (8, 10, 10) sts at beg of next row.

Place rem 11 sts on holder. Do not break yarn.

BACK

With WS facing, join yarn at underarm.

Work even for 1 row.

Keeping 1 st at each end in St st, [dec 1 st at each end every row] 3 (4, 5, 5) times. (36, 39, 43, 44 sts)

Work even until armhole measures 7½ (7½, 8, 8) inches above bound-off underarm sts, ending with a RS row.

Shape back neck

Work across 10 (11, 12, 12) sts, bind off next 16 (17, 19, 20) sts, join 2nd ball of yarn and work to end of row.

Work both sides of neck with separate balls of yarn, dec 1 st at each neck edge [every row] twice.

Bind off rem 8 (9, 10, 10) sts for each shoulder.

RIGHT FRONT

With WS facing, join yarn at underarm.

Work 1 row even.

Keeping 1 st at arm edge in St st, [dec 1 st at arm edge every row] 3 (4, 5, 5) times, *at the same time* dec 1 st before marker on this and every following 4th row 7 (7, 7, 8) times. (18, 19, 21, 21 sts)

Work even in pat until armhole measures 8½ (8½, 9, 9) inches above bound-off underarm sts, ending with a RS row.

Bind off 7 (8, 10, 10) sts at beg of next row.

Place rem 11 sts on holder. Do not break yarn.

Sew shoulder seams.

COLLAR

Sl sts of right front from holder to needle.

Keeping 1 st at neck edge in St st, work even in Seed pat until collar reaches center back of neck.

Place sts on holder; rep for left side of collar.

Sew center back seam of collar using Kitchener st (see page 170).

SLEEVES

Cast on 28 (33, 35, 36) sts using Cable cast-on technique.

Set up pat (WS): K1 for selvage st, p0 (1, 2, 4)-tbl, [k2-tbl, p6 (7, 7,

6)-tbl] 3 times, k2-tbl, p0 (1, 2, 4)-tbl, k1 for selvage st.

Working in Ladder pat, inc 1 st each end [every 6th (6th, 5th, 5th) row] 6 (6, 7, 8) times. (40, 45, 49, 52 sts)

Work even until sleeve measures 13½ (14, 14½, 14½) inches from beg, ending with a WS row.

Shape sleeve cap

Bind off 3 (4, 5, 5) sts at beg of next 2 rows.

Dec 1 st at each end [every row] 5 times, then [every other row] (6, 7, 8, 9) times. (12, 13, 14, 14 sts)

Bind off 3 (3, 3, 4) sts at beg of next 2 rows.

Bind off rem 6 (7, 8, 6) sts

BUTTONS
Make 6

With 2 strands of yarn held tog, cast on 1 st leaving a 4-inch end.

Row 1: Knit, purl, knit into same st. (3 sts)

Row 2: [K1, M1] 3 times. (6 sts)

Row 3: [K1, p1] 3 times.

Row 4: [K2tog] 3 times. (3 sts)

Row 5: K3tog.

Cut yarn leaving a 4-inch end.

Draw end through last st.

Tie tails tightly tog to form a bobble.

ASSEMBLY

Sew lower edge of collar to back neck.

Sew sleeves into armhole, matching shaping.

Sew sleeve seams.

Sew on buttons to correspond to buttonholes. ■

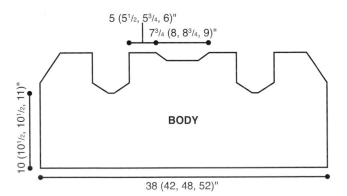

5 (5½, 5¾, 6)"

7¾ (8, 8¾, 9)"

10 (10½, 10½, 11)"

BODY

38 (42, 48, 52)"

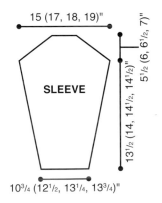

15 (17, 18, 19)"

5½ (6, 6½, 7)"

SLEEVE

13½ (14, 14½, 14½)"

10¾ (12½, 13¼, 13¾)"

CELTIC KNOT PULLOVER

Design by Melissa Leapman

Large Celtic knots embellish the front of an updated Aran-style pullover.

SIZE

Woman's small (medium, large, extra-large, 2X-large) Instructions are given for smallest size, with larger sizes in parentheses. When only 1 number is given, it applies to all sizes.

SKILL LEVEL
INTERMEDIATE
YARN WEIGHT
6 SUPER BULKY

FINISHED MEASUREMENTS

Chest: 37 (40, 43, 46, 49½) inches
Length: 24 (24½, 24½, 24½, 24½) inches

MATERIALS

- Plymouth Yukon 35 percent mohair/35 percent wool/30 percent acrylic super bulky weight yarn (59 yds/100g per ball): 11 (12, 13, 13, 14) balls natural #70
- Size 15 (10mm) needles or size needed to obtain gauge
- Cable needle
- Stitch markers and holders

GAUGE

10 sts and 12 rows = 4 inches/10cm in rev St st

To save time, take time to check gauge.

PATTERN STITCH
1/1 Rib
Row 1 (RS): K1, p1; rep from * across.

Rep Rows 1 for pat.

PATTERN NOTE
One selvage st is included on each side. These sts are not reflected in final measurements.

BACK
Cast on 52 (56, 60, 64, 68) sts.

Work even in 1/1 Rib for 10 rows.

Change to rev St st, and work even until back measures 16½ (16, 16, 15½, 15½) inches, ending with a WS row.

Shape armholes
Bind off 2 (3, 3, 4, 5) sts at beg of next 2 rows.

[Dec 1 st each end every row] 5 (5, 7, 7, 7) times. (38, 40, 40, 42, 44 sts)

Work even until armhole measures 8 (8½, 8½, 9, 9) inches above bound-off underarm sts, ending with a WS row.

Shape shoulders
Bind off 5 (5, 5, 6, 7) sts at beg of next 2 rows, then 5 (6, 6, 6, 6) sts at beg of following 2 rows.

Bind off rem 18 sts.

FRONT
Cast on 52 (56, 60, 64, 68) sts.

Row 1 (RS): [K1, p1] 12 (13, 14, 15, 16) times, k4, [p1, k1] 12 (13, 14, 14, 16) times.

Row 2: Knit or purl the sts as they present themselves.

Row 3: [K1, p1] 12 (13,14, 15, 16) times, sl next 2 sts to cn and hold in back, k2, k2 from cn, [p1, k1] 12 (13, 14, 14, 16) times.

Row 4: Rep Row 2.

Rep Rows 1–4 once more; rep Rows 1 and 2.

Next Row (RS): P13 (15, 17, 19, 21), pm, work Row 1 of Celtic Knot chart over next 26 sts, pm, p13 (15, 17, 19, 21).

Keeping sts between markers in Celtic Knot pat as established, and rem sts in rev St st, work even until front measures approx 16½ (16, 16, 15½, 15½) inches, ending with a WS row.

Shape armholes
Bind off 2 (3, 3, 4, 5) sts at beg of next 2 rows.

[Dec 1 st each end every row] 5 (5, 7, 7, 7) times. (38, 40, 40, 42, 44 sts).

Work even until front measures approx 23 inches from beg, ending after Row 2 of Celtic Knot pat.

Shape neck
Removing markers, work across 13 (14, 14, 15, 16) sts, place next 12 sts on holder for front neck, join 2nd ball of yarn and work to end row.

Work both sides of neck with separate balls of yarn, bind off 3 sts at each neck edge.

Work even until armholes measure same as for back above bound-off underarm sts.

Bind off rem 10 (11, 11, 12, 13) sts for each shoulder.

SLEEVES
Cast on 26 sts.

Work even in 1/1 Rib for 10 rows.

Working in rev St st, [inc 1 st each end every other row] 0 (0, 0, 3, 3) times, [every 4th row] 5 (8, 8, 8, 8) times, then [every 6th row] 3 (1, 1, 0, 0) times. (42, 44, 44, 48, 48 sts)

Work even until sleeve measures 16 inches from beg, ending with a WS row.

Shape sleeve cap
Bind off 2 (3, 3, 4, 5) sts at beg of next 2 rows. (38, 38, 38, 40, 38 sts)

[Dec 1 st each end every other row] 0 (3, 3, 3, 4) times, then every row 15 (12, 12, 13, 11) times.

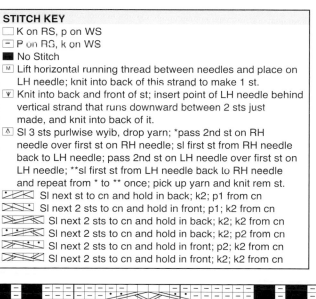

STITCH KEY
☐ K on RS, p on WS
⊟ P on RS, k on WS
■ No Stitch
Ⓜ Lift horizontal running thread between needles and place on LH needle; knit into back of this strand to make 1 st.
Ⓥ Knit into back and front of st; insert point of LH needle behind vertical strand that runs downward between 2 sts just made, and knit into back of it.
Ⓐ Sl 3 sts purlwise wyib, drop yarn; *pass 2nd st on RH needle over first st on RH needle; sl first st from RH needle back to LH needle; pass 2nd st on LH needle over first st on LH needle; **sl first st from LH needle back to RH needle and repeat from * to ** once; pick up yarn and knit rem st.
Sl next st to cn and hold in back; k2; p1 from cn
Sl next 2 sts to cn and hold in front; p1; k2 from cn
Sl next 2 sts to cn and hold in back; k2; k2 from cn
Sl next 2 sts to cn and hold in back; k2; p2 from cn
Sl next 2 sts to cn and hold in front; p2; k2 from cn
Sl next 2 sts to cn and hold in front; k2; k2 from cn

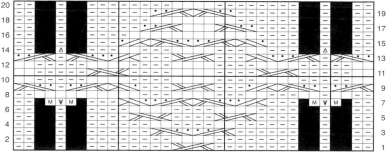

CELTIC KNOT PULLOVER

Bind off rem 8 sts.
Sew right shoulder seam.

COLLAR

With RS facing, pick up and knit 10 sts along left neck edge, sl front neck sts to LH needle, [k1, p1] twice, pm, k4, pm, [p1, k1] twice, pick up and knit 10 sts along right neck edge, and 18 sts along back neck. (50 sts)

Row 1 (WS): [P1, k1] to marker, p4, [k1, p1] to end of row.

Row 2: [K1, p1] to marker, sl next 2 sts to cn and hold in back, k2, k2 from cn, [p1, k1] to end of row.

Row 3: Rep Row 1.

Row 4: [K1, p1] to marker, p4, [p1, k1] to end of row.

Rep Rows 1–4 until collar measures 4 inches above picked-up row.

Bind off loosely in pat.

ASSEMBLY

Sew left shoulder seam, including side of collar.

Sew sleeves into armholes.
Sew sleeve and side seams. ■

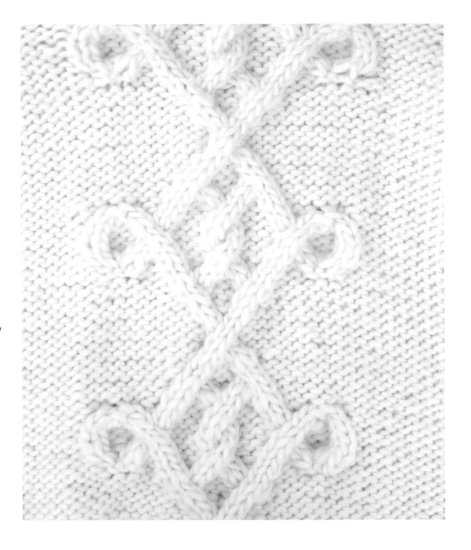

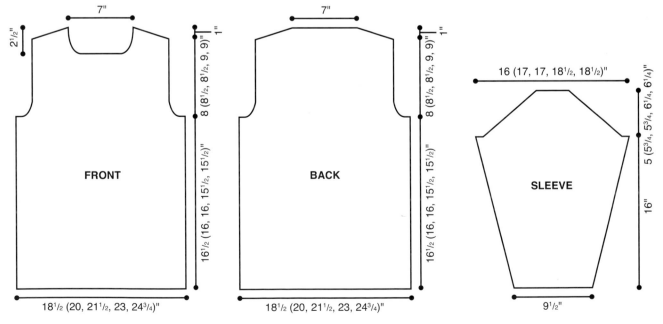

EASY-TO-WEAR LUSH TUNIC

Design by Gayle Bunn

Mohair yarn and a lacy pattern mix to form a soft, and very wearable tunic.

SIZE

Woman's small (medium, large, extra-large, 2X-large) Instructions are given for smallest size, with larger sizes in parentheses. When only 1 number is given, it applies to all sizes.

SKILL LEVEL
INTERMEDIATE

YARN WEIGHT
5 BULKY

FINISHED MEASUREMENTS

Chest: 38 (40, 42, 45, 47) inches
Length: 27 (27½, 27½, 28, 28½) inches

MATERIALS

- Plymouth Outback Mohair 70 percent mohair/26 percent wool/4 percent nylon bulky weight yarn (220 yds/100g per skein): 4 (4, 5, 5, 6) skeins blue/green variegated #801
- Size 11 (8mm) needles or size needed to obtain gauge
- Stitch holders

GAUGE

13 sts and 13 rows = 4 inches/10cm in Lace pat

To save time, take time to check gauge.

PATTERN STITCH

Lace (multiple of 4 sts + 1)

Row 1 (WS): Purl.

Row 2: K2tog, *(k1, yo, k1) in next st, sl 1, k2tog, psso; rep from * to last 3 sts, (k1, yo, k1) in next st, ssk.

Rep Rows 1 and 2 for pat.

BACK

Cast on 53 (57, 61, 65, 69) sts. Beg with a WS row, knit 6 rows, inc 8 sts evenly on last row. (61, 65, 69, 73, 77 sts)

Work even in Lace pat until back measures 18 inches, ending with a WS row.

Shape armholes

Bind off 8 sts at beg of next 2 rows. (45, 49, 53, 57, 61 sts)

Work even in established pat until armhole measures 8½ (9, 9, 9½, 10) inches above bound-off underarm sts, ending with a WS row.

Shape shoulders

Bind off 5 (6, 7, 8, 8) sts at beg of next 2 rows, then 6 (7, 7, 8, 9) sts at beg of following 2 rows.

Place rem 23 (23, 25, 25, 27) sts on holder.

FRONT

Work as for back until armhole measures 5½ (6, 6, 6½, 7) inches above bound-off underarm sts, ending with a WS row.

Shape neck

Work across 17 (19, 20, 22, 23) sts; place next 11 (11, 13, 13, 15) sts on holder for front neck; join 2nd ball of yarn and work to end of row.

Working on both sides of neck with separate balls of yarn, [dec 1 st at each neck edge every RS row] 6 times. (11, 13, 14, 16, 17 sts on each side of neck)

Work even until armhole measures same as for back above bound-off underarm sts.

Shape shoulders

Bind off at each arm edge, [5 (6, 7,

8, 8) sts] once, then [6 (7, 7, 8, 9) sts] once.

SLEEVES

Cast on 29 (31, 31, 33, 37) sts.

Beg with a WS row, knit 6 rows, inc 4 (6, 6, 8, 8) sts evenly on last row. (33, 37, 37, 41, 45 sts)

Working in Lace pat, [inc 1 st each end every 4th row] 13 times, working added sts into pat. (59, 63, 63, 67, 71 sts)

Work even until sleeve measures 18 (18, 18½, 18½, 19) inches from beg, ending with a WS row.

Place markers at each end of last row for underarm.

Work 8 rows even.

Shape sleeve cap

Bind off 8 (9, 9, 9, 10) at beg next 6 rows.

Bind off rem 11 (9, 9, 13, 11) sts.

COLLAR

Sew right shoulder seam.

With RS facing, pick up and knit 12 sts along left neck edge, k11 (11, 13, 13, 15) sts from front holder, pick up and knit 12 sts along right neck edge, k23 (23, 25, 25, 27) sts from back holder dec 1 st at center. (57, 57, 61, 61, 65 sts)

Work even in Lace pat until collar measures 9 inches, ending with a WS row.

Bind off.

ASSEMBLY

Sew left shoulder and collar seam. Fold collar in half to WS and sew to neck edge.

Sew sleeves into armholes, matching underarm markers to first bound-off underarm st of body.

Sew sleeve seams.

Measure 6 inches up from lower edge on side seams of front and back; mark.

Sew side seams, leaving area below markers open.

SIDE SLIT EDGING

Beg at cast-on edge with RS facing, pick up and knit 16 sts along side opening of front and 16 sts along side opening of back. (32 sts)

Bind off knitwise on WS.

Rep for opening on opposite side. ■

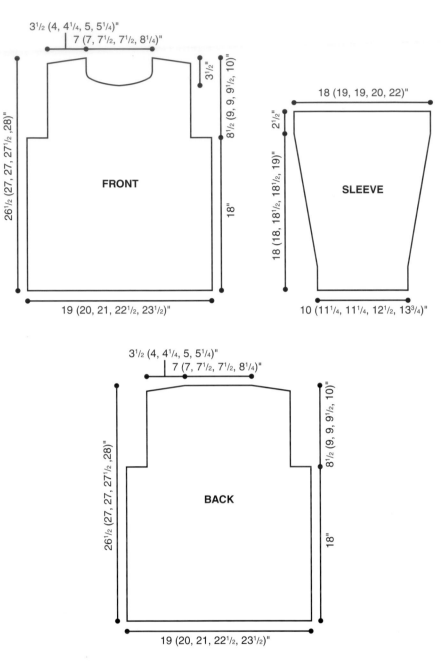

EVENING GLITZ PARTY JACKET

Design by Melissa Leapman

Add sparkle and glamour to your evening out with a glittery jacket.

SIZE

Woman's small (medium, large, extra-large, 2X-large) Instructions are given for smallest size, with larger sizes in parentheses. When only 1 number is given, it applies to all sizes.

SKILL LEVEL
EASY

YARN WEIGHT
5
BULKY

FINISHED MEASUREMENTS

Chest: 36 (40, 44, 48, 52) inches
Length: 20 (20½, 20½, 21, 21) inches

MATERIALS

- Plymouth Outback Mohair 70 percent mohair/26 percent wool/4 percent nylon bulky weight yarn (200 yds/100g per skeins): 4 (5, 5, 6, 6) skeins plum print #859 (A)
- Plymouth Glitterlash 50 percent polyester/50 percent metallic novelty eyelash carry-along yarn (185 yds/25 g per ball): 4 (5, 5, 6, 6) balls pink glitter #2 (B)
- Plymouth Colorlash 100 percent polyester novelty eyelash carry-along yarn (220 yds/50g per ball): 4 (5, 5, 6, 6) balls green #215 (C)
- Size 13 (9mm) needles or size needed to obtain gauge
- Size K/10½/6.5mm crochet hook;
- 1 (⅞-inch) button, JHB International #12219

GAUGE

8 sts and 12 rows = 4 inches/ 10cm in garter st

To save time, take time to check gauge.

PATTERN NOTES

One strand each of A, B and C are held tog throughout.

One selvage st at each side is included in pat. These sts are not reflected in final measurements.

BACK

With 1 strand each of A, B and C held tog, cast on 38 (42, 46, 50, 54) sts.

Work even in garter st until back measures 2 inches from beg, ending with a WS row.

Shape sides

Dec 1 st each end on next, then [every 4th row] twice. (32, 36, 40, 44, 48 sts)

Work even until back measures 6 inches, ending after a WS row.

Inc 1 st each end on next, then [every 4th row] twice. (38, 42, 46, 50, 54 sts)

Work even until back measures 10½ inches, ending after a WS row.

Shape armholes

Bind off 4 (4, 6, 6, 8) sts at beg of next two rows. (30, 34, 34, 38, 38 sts)

Work even until armhole measures 8½ (9, 9, 9½, 9½) inches above bound-off underarm sts, ending after WS row.

Shape Shoulders

Bind off 4 (5, 5, 6, 6) sts at beg of next 4 rows.

Bind off rem 14 sts.

LEFT FRONT

With 1 strand each of A, B and C held tog, cast on 19 (21, 23, 25, 27) sts.

Work even in garter st until back measures 2 inches from beg, ending with a WS row.

Shape side

Dec 1 st at arm edge on next, then

[every 4th row] twice. (16, 18, 20, 22, 24 sts)

Work even until back front 6 inches, ending after a WS row. Inc 1 st at arm edge on next, then [every 4th row] twice. (19, 21, 23, 25, 27 sts)

Work even until front mea-sures same as for back to under-arm, ending after a WS row.

Shape armhole

Bind off 4 (4, 6, 6, 8) sts at beg of next row. (15, 17, 17, 19, 19 sts)

Work even until armhole measures 6½ (7, 7, 7½, 7½) inches above bound-off underarm sts, ending with a RS row.

Shape neck

Bind off at neck edge [3 sts] once, then [2 sts] once.

[Dec 1 st at neck edge every row] twice. (8, 10, 10, 12, 12 sts)

Work even until armhole measures same as for back above bound-off underarm sts, ending with a WS row.

Shape shoulders

Bind off at arm edge 4 (5, 5, 6, 6) sts twice.

RIGHT FRONT

With 1 strand each of A, B and C held tog, cast on 19 (21, 23, 25, 27) sts.

Work even in garter st until back measures 2 inches from beg, ending with a WS row.

Shape side

Dec 1 st at arm edge on next, then [every 4th row] twice. (16, 18, 20, 22, 24 sts)

Work even until back front 6 inches, ending after a WS row.

Inc 1 st at arm edge on next, then [every 4th row] twice. (19, 21, 23, 25, 27 sts)

Work even until front measures same as for back to underarm, ending after a RS row.

Shape armhole

Bind off 4 (4, 6, 6, 8) sts at beg of next row. (15, 17, 17, 19, 19 sts)

Work even until armhole measures 6½ (7, 7, 7½, 7½) inches above bound-off underarm sts, ending with a WS row.

Shape neck

Bind off at neck edge [3 sts] once, then [2 sts] once.

[Dec 1 st at neck edge every row] twice. (8, 10, 10, 12, 12 sts)

Work even until armhole measures same as for back above

bound-off underarm sts, ending with a RS row.

Shape shoulders

Bind off at arm edge 4 (5, 5, 6, 6) sts twice.

SLEEVES

With 1 strand each of A, B, and C held tog, cast on 20 sts.

Working in garter st, [inc 1 st each end every 6th row] 0 (1, 2, 8, 10) times, [every 8th row] 3 (8, 7, 2, 0) times, then [every 10th row] 5 (0, 0, 0, 0) times. (36, 38, 38, 40, 40 sts)

Work even until sleeve measures 21½ (20½, 21, 20, 20) inches from beg.

Bind off.

Measure 2 (2, 3, 3, 4) inches from top edge and mark each end st for underarm.

Sew shoulder seams.

FRONT EDGING

Note: *If not familiar with single crochet st, refer to page 170.*

With RS facing and crochet hook, attach yarn with sl st to lower right front edge, ch 1.

Row 1 (RS): Making sure to keep work flat, work 1 row of sc up right front, around neck, and down left front, working 3 sc in each corner neck st, turn.

Row 2: Ch 1, sc in each sc, skipping 3 sts and working a ch-3 for buttonhole at top of right neck.

Fasten off.

ASSEMBLY

Sew sleeves into armholes matching underarm markers to first bound-off underarm st of body.

Sew sleeve and side seams. Sew on button. ■

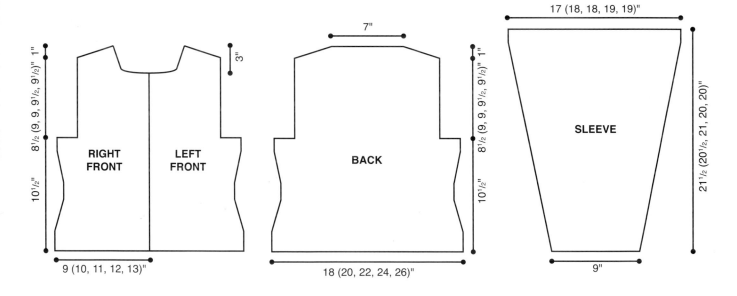

SO PRECIOUS CHILD'S A-LINE JACKET

Design by Kennita Tully

Bright handpainted bouclé and soft alpaca combine in a jacket for a precious little girl.

SIZE
Girl's 2 (4, 6, 8) Instructions are given for smallest size, with larger sizes in parentheses. When only 1 number is given, it applies to all sizes

MC

CC

FINISHED MEASUREMENTS
Chest (buttoned): 25 (27, 29, 32) inches
Length: 15½ (16½, 17½, 18½) inches

MATERIALS
- Plymouth Rimini Rainbow 60 percent acrylic/40 percent wool super bulky weight yarn (38 yds/50g per ball): 6 (7, 8, 9) balls purple rainbow #27 (MC)
- Plymouth Baby Alpaca Brush 80 percent baby alpaca/20 percent acrylic bulky weight yarn (110 yds/50g per ball): 1 ball light green #1477 (CC)
- Size 11 (8mm) straight and 16-inch circular needle
- Size 15 (10mm) needles or size needed to obtain gauge
- Stitch markers
- 3 (1-inch) buttons

GAUGE

7 sts and 16 rows = 4 inches/10cm in garter st with larger needles

To save time, take time to check gauge.

PATTERN NOTE

Two strands of CC yarn are held tog for entire garment.

BACK

With MC and larger needles, cast on 28 (30, 32, 34) sts.

Working in garter stitch, dec 1 st at each end of Row 11 (13, 15, 13), then [every 14 (14, 14, 16) rows] twice. (22, 24, 26, 28 sts)

Place marker at each end of last row for underarm.

Work even until armhole measures 5½ (6, 6½, 7) inches above underarm markers.

Bind off all sts.

Mark center 12 (14, 16, 18) sts for back neck.

RIGHT FRONT

With MC and larger needles, cast on 13 (14, 15, 16) sts.

Working in garter stitch, dec 1 st at arm edge on Row 11 (13, 15, 13), then [every 14 (14, 14, 16) rows] twice. (10, 11, 12, 13 sts)

Place marker at last row for underarm.

Work even until armhole measures 3 (3½, 4, 4½) inches above underarm marker, ending with a WS row.

Shape neck

Bind off 3 (4, 4, 5) at beg of next row.

[Dec 1 st at neck edge every row] 2 (2, 3, 3) times. (5 sts)

Work even until armhole measures same as for back above underarm marker.

Bind off.

BUTTONHOLE BAND

With MC and larger needles, pick

up and knit 29 (31, 33, 35) sts along front edge.

Knit 3 rows.

Buttonhole row (RS): K15 (17, 19, 21) sts, [bind off 2 sts, k3] twice, bind off 2 sts, k2.

Next row: Knit, casting on 2 sts over each bound-off area.

Work even until band measures 1½ inches.

Bind off.

LEFT FRONT

With MC and larger needles, cast on 13 (14, 15, 16) sts.

Working in garter stitch, dec 1 st at arm edge on Row 11 (13, 15, 13), then [every 14 (14, 14, 16) rows] twice. (10, 11, 12, 13 sts)

Place marker at last row for underarm.

Work even until armhole measures 3 (3½, 4, 4½) inches

above underarm marker, ending with a RS row.

Shape neck

Bind off 3 (4, 4, 5) at beg of next row.

[Dec 1 st at neck edge every row] 2 (2, 3, 3) times. (5 sts)

Work even until armhole measures same as for back above underarm marker.

Bind off.

BUTTON BAND

With MC and larger needles, pick up and knit 29 (31, 33, 35) sts along front edge.

Work in garter st for 1½ inches.
Bind off.
Sew shoulder seams.

COLLAR

With smaller needles and RS facing, using 2 strands of CC held tog, pick up and knit 16 sts along right neck edge, 1 st in each bound off st of back neck, and 16 sts along left neck edge. (44, 46, 48, 50 sts)

Work even in rev St st until collar measures 3 inches.

Bind off loosely.

SLEEVES

With MC and larger needles, cast on 12 (12, 14, 14) sts.

Working in garter st, [inc 1 st each end every 8 (6, 6, 6) rows] 4 (5, 5, 6) times. (20, 22, 24, 26) sts.

Work even until sleeve measures 8½ (9, 9½, 10) inches.

Bind off loosely.

CUFF

With smaller needles and RS facing, using 2 strands of CC held tog, pick up and knit 12 (12, 14, 14) sts along cast-on edge of sleeve.

Work even in rev St st for 2 inches.

Bind off.

ASSEMBLY

Sew sleeves to body between underarm markers.

Sew sleeve and side seams.

Sew on buttons.

Tack collar to inside at neckline. ■

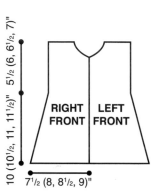

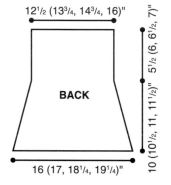

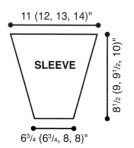

RELAXED & WARM LATTICE PULLOVER

Design by Celeste Pinheiro

A trellis pattern adds interest to a chunky outdoor sweater for the man in your life.

SIZE

Man's small (medium, large, extra-large) Instructions are given for smallest size, with larger sizes in parentheses. When only 1 number is given, it applies to all sizes.

SKILL LEVEL
INTERMEDIATE

YARN WEIGHT
6 SUPER BULKY

FINISHED MEASUREMENTS

Chest: 40 (44, 48, 52) inches
Length: 26 (26, 27, 27) inches

MATERIALS

- Plymouth Encore Mega 75 percent acrylic/25 percent wool super bulky weight yarn (64 yds/100g per skein): 12 (13, 13, 14) skeins beige #240
- Size 11 (8mm) straight and 16-inch circular needles
- Size 13 (9mm) needles or size needed to obtain gauge
- Cable needle (cn)

GAUGE

8 sts and 14 rows = 4 inches/10cm in St st using larger needles

10 sts and 14 rows = 4 inches/10cm in Lattice pat using larger needles

To save time, take time to check gauge.

PATTERN NOTE

Work sts in St st if there are not enough sts to work complete cable crossing at edge of piece.

BACK

With smaller needles cast on 50 (56, 60, 66) sts.

Work even in k1, p1 rib for 2 inches, ending with a WS row. Change to larger needles. Knit 1 row, purl 1 row.

Referring to chart, work even in Lattice pat until back measures 16½ (16½, 17, 17) inches from beg, ending with a WS row.

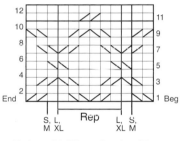

Relaxed & Warm Lattice Chart

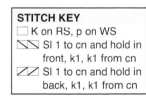

STITCH KEY
☐ K on RS, p on WS
◥◣ Sl 1 to cn and hold in
    front, k1, k1 from cn
◢◤ Sl 1 to cn and hold in
    back, k1, k1 from cn

Shape armholes

Bind of 6 sts at beg of next 2 rows. (38, 44, 48, 54 sts)

Work even until armhole measures 8½ (8½, 9, 9) inches above bound-off underarm sts, ending with a WS row.

Shape neck

Work across 10 (12, 14, 16) sts; join 2nd ball of yarn and bind off next 18 (20, 20, 22) sts for back neck; work to end of row.

Work both sides of neck with separate balls of yarn, dec 1 st at each neck edge once. (9, 11, 13, 15 sts on each side of neck)

Work even until armhole

measures 9½ (9½, 10, 10) inches.
Bind off shoulder sts.

FRONT

Work as for back until armhole measures 6½ (6½, 7, 7) inches above bound-off underarm sts.

Shape neck

Work across 15 (18, 20, 23) sts; join 2nd ball of yarn and bind off next 8 sts for front neck; work to end of row.

Work both sides of neck with separate balls of yarn, bind off at each neck edge [3 sts] 0 (0, 0, 1) time, [2 sts] 3 (3, 3, 2) times, then [1 st] 0 (1, 1, 1) time. (9, 11, 13, 15 sts on each side of neck)

Work even until armhole measures same as for back.
Sew shoulder seams.

NECKBAND

With RS facing and smaller circular needles, join yarn at back neck.

Knit across 18 (20, 20, 22) sts of back neck, pick up and knit 10 (11, 11, 12) sts along left neck edge, knit across 8 sts of front neck, pick up and knit 10 (11, 11, 12) sts along right neck edge. (46, 50, 50, 54 sts)

Pm between first and last st.
Work even in k1, p1 rib for 4 rnds.
Bind off loosely in rib.

SLEEVE

With smaller needles cast on 22 (22, 24, 24) sts.

Work even in k1, p1 rib for 2 inches, ending with a WS row.
Change to larger needles.

Working in St st, inc 1 st each end [every 6th row] 8 times. (38, 38, 40, 40 sts)

Work even until sleeve measures 19 (19, 18, 18) inches.

Mark each end st for underarm. Work even for 2 inches more. Bind off all sts.

ASSEMBLY

Sew sleeves into armholes, matching underarm markers to first bound-off underarm st of body.

Sew sleeve and side seams. ■

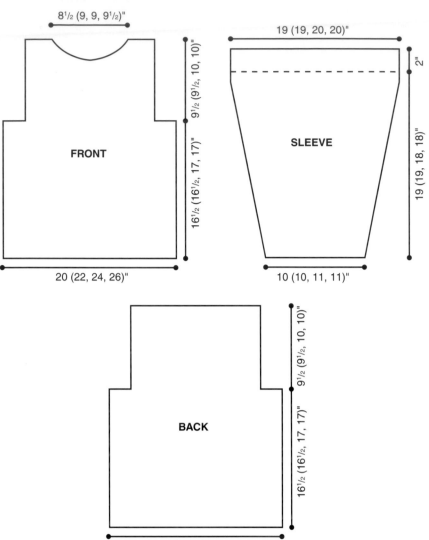

ZIP HOODIE FOR ACTIVE BOYS

Design by Celeste Pinheiro

Active boys love the comfort of this vest. Moms love the warmth it furnishes.

SIZE

Boy's 2 (4, 6, 8)
Instructions are given for smallest size, with larger sizes in parentheses. When only 1 number is given, it applies to all sizes.

SKILL LEVEL
INTERMEDIATE

YARN WEIGHT
6 SUPER BULKY

FINISHED MEASUREMENTS

Chest: 28 (30, 32, 34) inches
Length: 14 (15, 16, 17) inches, without hood

MATERIALS

- Plymouth Encore Mega 75 percent acrylic/25 percent wool super bulky weight yarn (64 yds/100g per skein): 4 (5, 5, 6) skeins blue #515
- Size 11 (8mm) needles
- Size 13 (9mm) needles or size needed to obtain gauge
- Cable needle
- Stitch holders
- 12 (12, 14, 14)-inch separating zipper
- Matching sewing thread

GAUGE

8 sts and 14 rows = 4 inches/10cm in St st with larger needles

10 sts and 14 rows = 4 inches/10cm in Lattice pat with larger needles

RADIO FLY

TOWN & COU

To save time, take time to check gauge.

PATTERN NOTE
Work sts in St st if there are not enough sts to work complete cable crossing at edge of piece.

POCKETS
Make 2
With larger needles cast on 10 (10, 12, 12) sts.

Work even in St st until piece measures 4 inches from beg.

Place sts on holder.

BACK
With smaller needles cast on 36 (38, 40, 42) sts.

Work even in k1, p1 rib for 2 inches, ending with a WS row. Change to larger needles. Knit 1 row, purl 1 row.

Referring to chart, work even in Lattice pat until back measures 8 (8½, 9, 9½) inches, ending with a WS row.

Shape armhole
Bind off 2 sts at beg of next 2 rows.

[Dec 1 st each end every other row] 4 times. (24, 26, 28, 30 sts)

Work even in established pattern until armhole measures 6 (6½, 7, 7½) inches above bound-off underarm sts.

Bind off.

LEFT FRONT
With smaller needles cast on 18 (19, 20, 21) sts.

Work even in k1, p1 rib for 2 inches, ending with a WS row. Change to larger needles. Knit 1 row, purl 1 row.

Referring to chart, work even in Lattice pat until front measures 6 inches, ending with a RS row.

Insert pocket
Next row (WS): P3, bind off 10 (10, 12, 12) sts knitwise, purl to end of row.

Row 2: Work in established pat across first 5 (6, 5, 6) sts, work 10 (10, 12, 12) pocket sts from holder, work to end of row.

Work even until front measures same as for back to underarm, ending with a WS row.

Shape underarm
Bind off 2 sts at beg of next row. [Dec 1 st at arm edge every other row] 4 times. (12, 13, 14, 15 sts)

Work even until armhole measures 4 (4½, 5, 5½) inches above bound-off underarm sts, ending with a RS row.

Shape neck
Bind off 4 (4, 5, 5) sts at neck edge.

[Dec 1 st at neck edge every other row] 4 times. (4, 5, 5, 6 sts)

Work even until armhole measures same as for back.

Bind off.

RIGHT FRONT
With smaller needles cast on 18 (19, 20, 21) sts.

Work even in k1, p1 rib for 2 inches, ending with a WS row. Change to larger needles. Knit 1 row, purl 1 row.

Referring to chart, work even in Lattice pat until front measures 6 inches, ending with a RS row.

Insert pocket
Next row (WS): P5 (6, 5, 6) sts, bind off 10 (10, 12, 12) sts knitwise, purl to end of row.

Row 2: Work in established pat across first 3 sts, work 10 (10, 12, 12) pocket sts from holder, work to end of row.

Work even until front measures same as for back to underarm, ending with a RS row.

Shape underarm
Bind off 2 sts at beg of next row.

[Dec 1 st at arm edge every other row] 4 times. (12, 13, 14, 15 sts)

Work even until armhole measures 4 (4½, 5, 5½) inches above bound-off underarm sts, ending with a WS row.

Shape neck

Bind off 4 (4, 5, 5) sts at neck edge.

[Dec 1 st at neck edge every other row] 4 times. (4, 5, 5, 6 sts)

Work even until armhole measures same as for back.

Bind off.

HOOD

With larger needles cast 34 (36, 38, 40) sts.

Work even in St st until hood measures 3 (3, 3½, 3½) inches from beg, ending with a WS row. [Inc 1 st each end every other row] 4 times. (42, 44, 46, 48 sts)

Work even until hood measures 7 (7, 8, 8) inches from beg.

Place sts on piece of yarn.

ASSEMBLY

Sew shoulder seams.

Fold hood in half and sew cast-on edges tog for back seam. Sew shaped edge of hood to neckline, matching center back and front edges.

ARMBAND

With RS facing and smaller needles, pick up and knit 36 (38, 42, 44) sts evenly around armhole.

Knit 1 row.

Bind off.

FRONT EDGING

With RS facing and smaller needles, pick up and knit 30 (32, 34, 36) sts along right front edge, sl sts from yarn holder to LH needle and knit them, pick up and knit 30 (32, 34, 36) sts along left front edge. (102, 108, 114, 120 sts)

Knit 1 row.

Bind off all sts.

FINISHING

Sew side seams.

Sew pockets to inside.

Sew in zipper. ■

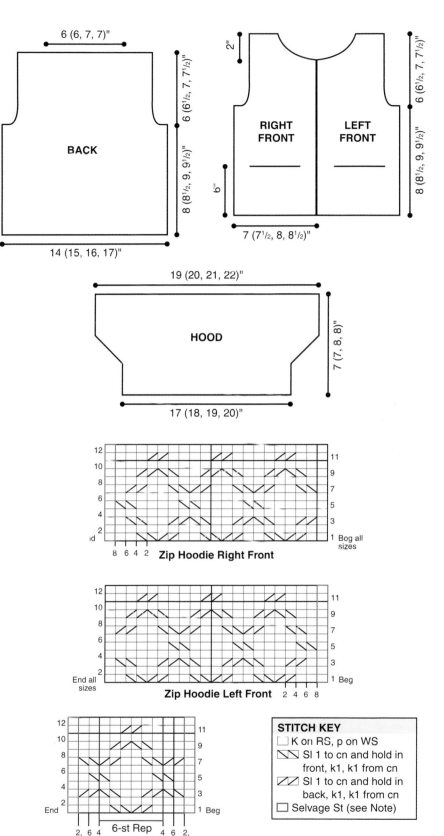

Zip Hoodie Right Front

Zip Hoodie Left Front

Zip Hoodie Back

STITCH KEY
☐ K on RS, p on WS
⟍⟍ Sl 1 to cn and hold in front, k1, k1 from cn
⟋⟋ Sl 1 to cn and hold in back, k1, k1 from cn
☐ Selvage St (see Note)

Note: Work first and last sts (selvages) in St st, then beg and end where indicated on the chart. If there are not 2 sts to work cable at edge before the selvage st, work in St st.

STYLISH WRAPS

These chill-chasing ponchos, capes and shawls come in handy over shoulder-baring fashions or any time an extra layer is needed for comfort.

RAINBOWS IN THE SNOW CAPELET

Design by Gayle Bunn

A shawl collar graces a short, kaleidoscopic cape.

SKILL LEVEL
■■□□
EASY

YARN WEIGHT
4
MEDIUM
A

YARN WEIGHT
6
SUPER BULKY
B & D

YARN WEIGHT
5
BULKY
C

SIZE
Woman's small/large (extra-large/
2X-large) Instructions are given
for smaller size, with larger size in
parentheses. When only 1 number
is given, it applies to both sizes.

FINISHED MEASUREMENT
Length: 18 inches

MATERIALS
- Plymouth Rimini Rainbow 60
  percent acrylic/40 percent wool
  super bulky weight yarn (38 yds/
  50g per ball): 8 (9) balls rainbow
  white #10 (MC)
- Plymouth Flash 100 percent
  nylon worsted weight eyelash
  yarn (190 yds/50g per ball): 2
  balls white #900 (A)
- Plymouth Baby Alpaca Brush 80
  percent baby alpaca/20 percent
  acrylic (110 yds/50g per ball): 1
  ball soft white #1000 (B)
- Size 11 (8mm) needles 36-inch
  circular needle
- Size 15 (10mm) 36-inch circular
  needle or size needed to obtain
  gauge

- Stitch holders
- Stitch markers
- 3 (1-inch) buttons
- 2 sets large snap fasteners
- Size H/8 (5mm) crochet hook

GAUGE
8 sts and 12 rows = 4 inches/
10cm in rev St st with larger needle
and MC.

To save time, take time to
check gauge.

PATTERN NOTES
Circular needle is used to accommodate large number of sts.

Do not join; work in rows.

CAPELET

LOWER FRONT SECTION
Make 2
With MC and larger needle, cast on
20 (22) sts.

Work even in rev St st for 7
rows, ending with a WS row.

Place sts on holder; do not cut
yarn of 2nd section.

MAIN SECTION
With MC and larger needle, cast
on 72 (76) sts.

Work even in rev St st for 7
rows, ending with a WS row.

Cut yarn.

Join sections
Next row: Purl across 20 (22) sts
of 2nd front section, 72 (76) sts of
main section, and 20 (22) sts of
rem front section. (112, 120 sts)

Work even until cape measures
8½ inches, ending with a WS row.

Beg shoulder shaping
Row 1 (RS): P28 (29), p2tog, p1
and mark this st, p2tog, p46 (52),
p2tog, p1 and mark this st, p2tog,
p28 (29).

Row 2: Knit.

Row 3: [Purl to 2 sts before
marked st, p2tog, purl marked st,
p2tog] twice, purl to end of row.

Row 4: Knit.

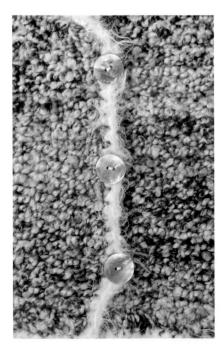

Beg neck shaping

Row 1: P2tog, [purl to 2 sts before marked st, p2tog, purl marked st, p2tog] twice, purl to last 2 sts, p2tog.

Row 2: K2tog, knit to last 2 sts, k2tog.

Dec 1 st at each front edge on next 4 rows, *at the same time*, dec at shoulders as before on next and following RS row. (80, 88 sts)

[Dec 1 st at each front edge and 2 sts at each shoulder marker every RS row] 6 (3) times. (44, 70 sts)

Next row (WS): [Knit to 2 sts before marked st, k2tog, knit marked st, k2tog] twice, knit to end of row.

Row 2: P2tog, *[purl to 2 sts before marked st, p2tog, purl marked st, p2tog] twice, purl to last 2 sts, p2tog.

Rep last 2 rows 0 (3) times more. (34, 30 sts)

Next row (WS): [Knit to 2 sts before marked st, k2tog, knit marked st, k2tog] twice, knit to end of row.

Row 2: [Purl to 2 sts before marked st, p2tog, purl marked st, p2tog] twice, purl to end of row.

Rep last 2 rows 1 (0) time more. (18, 22 sts)

For size small/large only

Place rem sts on holder.

For size extra-large/2X-large only

Next row (WS): [Knit to 2 sts before marked st, k2tog, knit marked st, k2tog] twice, knit to end of row. (18 sts)

Place rem sts on holder.

COLLAR

With smaller needle and RS facing, using 2 strands of A and 1 strand of B held tog, pick up and knit 34 (38) sts along right neck edge, knit 18 sts of back neck, pick up and knit 34 (38) sts along left neck edge. (86, 94 sts)

Knit 1 row.

Next 2 rows: [Knit to last 2 sts, turn] twice.

*Knit to 2 sts before previous turning st, turn; rep from * until there are 24 (26) unworked sts at each end of needle (38 sts in center).

Knit 2 rows, working across all sts.

Bind off.

EDGING

Note: *If not familiar with single crochet st, refer to page 173.*

Row 1 (RS): With RS facing, join MC at neck edge of left front. Work 1 row of sc down left front, across bottom edges including slits, and up right front, making sure to keep work flat and working 3 sc in each outer corner and dec 1 st at top of each front slit.

Fasten off.

Mark positions for 3 button lps on right front having bottom button 2 inches above lower edge, top button 1 inch below neck edge and rem button spaced evenly between.

Row 2: With RS facing, join 2 strands of A and 1 strand of B with sl st to corner of lower left front, ch 1, work 1 sc in each sc of previous row working 3 sc at each outer corner and dec 1 st at top of each front slit. At each buttonhole marker work (ch 3, sk next 2 sc, sc in next sc).

Fasten off.

ASSEMBLY

Lap 8 inches of right front over left front and mark position for buttons on right front.

Mark for first snap on inside at top corner of left neck; mark for 2nd snap 5 inches below first, along left front edge.

Sew buttons and snaps in position. ∎

VERY EASY, VERY COZY RUANA

Design by Katharine Hunt

Three strands of yarn combine to create a soft and cozy garment that's easy to knit.

SIZE

Woman's extra-small/small (medium/large) Instructions are given for smallest size, with larger size in parentheses. When only 1 number is given, it applies to both sizes.

SKILL LEVEL
EASY

YARN WEIGHT
4 MEDIUM

FINISHED MEASUREMENTS

Width: 27 (31) inches
Length: 26½ (30) inches

MATERIALS

- Plymouth Encore Worsted 75 percent acrylic/25 percent wool worsted weight yarn (200 yds/100g per skein): 4 (5) skeins beige heather #240 (A)
- Plymouth Encore Colorspun Worsted 75 percent acrylic/25 percent wool worsted weight yarn (200 yds/100g per skein): 4 (5) skeins peach variegated #7123 (B)
- Plymouth Imperiale Super Kid Mohair 80 percent mohair/20 percent nylon worsted weight yarn (109 yds/25g per ball): 8 (9) balls green variegated #4123 (C)
- Size 13 (9mm) 30-inch circular needles or size needed to obtain gauge
- Size L/11 (8mm) crochet hook

GAUGE

11 sts and 15 rows = 4 inches/10cm in pat st.

To save time, take time to check gauge.

SPECIAL ABBREVIATION

W&T (Wrap & Turn): Bring yarn to front of work, sl next st purlwise, take yarn to back of work, return sl st to LH needle.

PATTERN STITCH

Long Basket Weave
(multiple of 6 sts +2)

Row 1 (RS): *K2, p4; rep from * to last 2 sts, k2.

Row 2: *P2, k4; rep from * to last 2 sts, p2.

Rows 3–6: Rep Rows 1 and 2.

Row 7: P3, *k2, p4; rep from * to last 5 sts, k2, p3.

Row 8: K3, *p2, k4; rep from * to last 5 sts, p2, k3.

Rows 9–12: Rep Rows 7 and 8.
Rep Rows 1–12 for pat.

PATTERN NOTES

Circular needle is used to accommodate large number of sts. Do not join; work in rows.

One strand each of A, B, and C are held tog throughout garment.

One strand each of A and B are held tog for crochet edging.

BACK

With 1 strand of each yarn held tog, cast on 74 (86) sts.

Knit 4 rows.

Work even in Long Basket Weave pat until back measures 23½ (27) inches, ending with a RS row.

Shape shoulders

Bind off at each arm edge [5 (7) sts] 1 (2) times, then [6 sts] 3 (2) times. (28, 34 sts)

LEFT FRONT

With 1 strand of each yarn held tog, cast on 38 (44) sts.

Knit 4 rows.

Work even in Long Basket Weave pat until back measures 12½ (14½) inches, ending with a WS row.

Shape neck

Work in established pat to last 2 sts, k2tog.

Continue to dec 1 st at neck edge [every 4th row] 14 (17) times more. (23, 26 sts)

Work even until front measures same as for back to shoulder, ending with a WS row.

Shape shoulder

Bind off at arm edge [5 (7) sts] 1 (2) times, then [6 sts] 3 (2) times.

RIGHT FRONT

With 1 strand of each yarn held tog, cast on 38 (44) sts.

Knit 4 rows.

Work even in Long Basket Weave pat until back measures 12½ (14½) inches, ending with a WS row.

Shape neck

Work in established pat to last 2 sts, ssk.

Continue to dec 1 st at neck edge [every 4th row] 14 (17) times more. (23, 26 sts)

Work even until front measures same as for back to shoulder, ending with a RS row.

Shape shoulder

Bind off at arm edge [5 (7) sts] 1 (2) times, then [6 sts] 3 (2) times.

Sew shoulder seams.

EDGING

Note: *If not familiar with single crochet st, refer to page 173.*

With crochet hook and 1 strand each of A and B held tog, beg at lower right front, work 1 sc in every other row along right front edge, around back neck and along left front edge, making sure to keep work flat.

Fasten off.

Rep edging along each side edge. ■

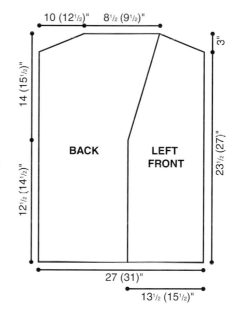

SPICE-UP-YOUR-WARDROBE SHAWL

Design by Pauline Schultz

A soft and scrumptious wrap in Mardi Gras colors will add a spicy touch to your wardrobe.

SIZE

Approx 24 x 70 inches, excluding fringe

SKILL LEVEL
EASY

YARN WEIGHT
5 BULKY

MATERIALS

- Plymouth Outback Mohair 70 percent mohair/26 percent wool/4 percent nylon (218 yards/100g per skein): 3 skeins Mardi Gras #895
- Size 13 (9mm) circular needle
- Stitch markers
- Size I/9 (5.5mm) crochet hook

GAUGE

Gauge is not critical for this project.

SPECIAL ABBREVIATION

K2w: Insert RH needle into next st, wrap yarn around needle twice, pull both wraps through st.

PATTERN NOTES

Sl all stitches purlwise.

When joining a new strand of yarn, place it parallel to yarn in use and work 3 or 4 stitches with both yarns, then continue with new ball.

After washing and blocking, trim ends.

SHAWL

Loosely cast on 56 sts.

Set up pat: Sl 1, *[k2w, sl 1 wyif,

take yarn to back of work] 3 times, pm, [ssk, yo] 3 times, pm; rep from * 3 times, [k2w, sl 1 wyif, take yarn to back of work] 3 times, k1.

Pat row: Sl 1, *[k2w, sl 1 wyif dropping extra wrap, take yarn to back of work] 3 times, [ssk, yo] 3 times; rep from *, end last rep k2w, sl 1 wyif dropping extra wrap, take yarn to back of work, k1.

Rep Pat row until shawl measures 70 inches.

Bind off very loosely.

FRINGE

Following Fringe instructions on page 170, make single knot fringe. Cut 14-inch strands of yarn.

With 6 strands held tog place knot in every other st along cast-on edge.

Rep along bound-off edge.

Trim fringe ends to 6 inches. ■

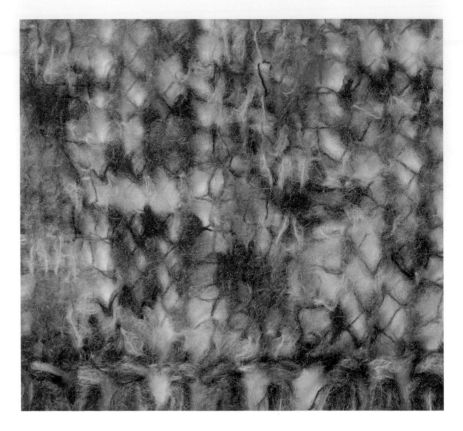

PERUVIAN LACE CABLE SHAWL

Design by Barbara Venishnick

Thanks to the special baby alpaca yarn, this shawl is lighter than air. It's just the thing for a cool summer evening, or a splash of color over a winter coat.

SIZE

Approx 22 x 72 inches, excluding fringe

SKILL LEVEL
INTERMEDIATE

YARN WEIGHT
5
BULKY

MATERIALS

- Plymouth Baby Alpaca Brush 80 percent baby alpaca/20 percent acrylic bulky weight yarn (110 yds/50g per ball): 7 balls rust #105
- Size 11 (8mm) 29-inch circular needle or size needed to obtain gauge
- Cable needle

GAUGE

14 stitches and 16 rows = 4 inches/10cm in Lace Cable pat

To save time, take time to check gauge.

PATTERN STITCH

Lace Cable (multiple of 14 sts + 8)

Row 1 (RS): K2, *yo, ssk, k2tog, yo, k3, yo, ssk, k2tog, yo, k3; rep from * to last 6 sts, yo, ssk, k2tog, yo, k2.

Row 2 and all WS rows: Purl.

Rows 3 and 5: Rep Row 1.

Row 7: K2, *yo, ssk, k2tog, yo, sl 3 sts to cn and hold in front, k2, k3 from cn, sl 2 sts to cn and hold in back, k3, k2 from cn; rep from * to last 6 sts, yo, ssk, k2tog, k2.

Rows 9 and 11: Rep Row 1.

Row 13: Rep Row 7.

Rows 15 and 17: Rep Row 1.

Row 18: Purl

PATTERN NOTE

Circular needle is used to accommodate large number of sts.

Do not join; work in rows.

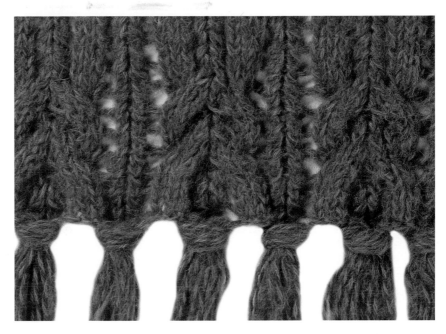

SHAWL

Cast on 78 stitches.

    [Work Rows 1–18 of Lace Cable pat] 14 times.

    Rep Rows 1–5.

    Loosely bind off knitwise on WS.

FRINGE

Following Fringe instructions on page 173, make single knot fringe. Cut 12-inch strands of yarn.

    Holding 10 strands tog, fold each group in half. Working along cast-on edge, place knot at center of each dec ridge and center of each cable.

    Rep along bound-off edge.

    Trim fringe evenly. ■

GO-WITH-EVERYTHING PONCHO

Design by Lois S. Young

The name says it all for this trendy accessory. Wear it over jeans or a little black party dress; this is a poncho that will fit in anywhere.

SIZE
Woman's—One size fits most

SKILL LEVEL
BEGINNER

YARN WEIGHT
5 BULKY

FINISHED MEASUREMENTS
Approx 19 x 50 inches, before sewing

MATERIALS
• Plymouth Furlauro 100 percent nylon bulky eyelash yarn (85 yds/ 50g per ball): 10 balls purple/ green/blue mix #828
• Size 11 (8mm) needles or size needed to obtain gauge

GAUGE
14 sts and 17 rows = 4 inches/ 10cm in garter st

To save time, take time to check gauge.

PATTERN NOTES
Count sts frequently, as it is very easy to lose a st in this highly textured yarn.

Poncho can be worn with point at center front, side, or in back.

PONCHO
Cast on 64 sts.

All rows: Sl 1p wyif, knit to end of row.

Work even until piece measures 50 inches from beg.

Bind off.

ASSEMBLY
Sew bound-off edge to side to right of cast-on edge (Fig. 1).

Fluff out 'fur' caught in seam. ∎

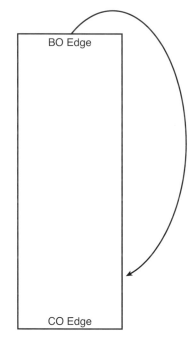

BO Edge

CO Edge

Fig. 1

EASY ELONGATED STITCH PONCHO

Design by Cindy Polfer

This elegant poncho knits up quickly, which means you are ready to go in no time at all.

SIZE
Woman's small/medium (large/extra-large, 2X-large/3X-large) Instructions are given for smallest size, with larger sizes in parentheses. When only 1 number is given, it applies to all sizes.

SKILL LEVEL
INTERMEDIATE
YARN WEIGHT
4
MEDIUM

SKILL LEVEL
INTERMEDIATE
YARN WEIGHT
5
BULKY

MATERIALS
• Plymouth Outback Mohair 70 percent mohair/26 percent wool/4 percent nylon bulky weight yarn (220 yds/100g per skein): 1 (1, 2) skeins blue variegated #896
• Plymouth Outback Wool 100 percent virgin wool worsted weight yarn (374 yds/200g per hank): 1 hank purple/blue variegated #996 (A)
• Plymouth Electra 100 percent nylon worsted weight novelty yarn (125 yds/50g per ball): 1 (1, 2) balls shades of denim #15 (B)
• Size 13 (9mm) needles or size needed to obtain gauge
• Stitch markers

GAUGE
8 sts and 9 rows = 4 inches/10cm in Elongated Loop pat
Row gauge may vary as the elongated rows created by the yo's should have many fewer rows per 4" in comparison with the stitch gauge.
To save time, take time to check gauge.

PATTERN STITCH
Elongated Loop
Row 1 (RS): With 1 strand each MC & B held tog, k1, *yo twice, k1; rep from * across row.
Row 2: Knit, dropping all yo's from needle.
Rows 3 and 4: With 1strand each MC & A held tog, knit.
Rep Rows 1–4 for pat.

PATTERN NOTES
Poncho is worked with 2 strands of yarn indicated held tog throughout.
Elongated st is made by working a double yo, then dropping extra wraps on the following row. After working Row 2, gently tug stitches to lengthen them.
Carry yarn not in use along edge, catching it into the last st worked on rows 2 and 4.
Inc are worked by knitting into front and back of a st.
Dec are worked by using ssk.

PONCHO
With 1 strand each MC & A held tog, cast on 29 (30, 31) sts.

Knit 2 rows.
*[Work Rows 1–4 of Elongated Loop pat] 5 (6, 7) times, inc 1 st at beg of Row 3 on each pat rep. (34, 36, 38 sts)
Rep Rows 1–4, without inc.
Mark last st for shoulder.
[Work Rows 1–4 of Elongated Loop pat] 5 (5, 6) times, dec 1 st at beg of Row 3 on each pat rep. (29, 31, 32 sts)*
[Rep Rows 1–4] 1 (2, 1) times, without inc.
Rep from * to * once.
Rep Rows 1–4, without inc.
With one strand each MC & B held tog, bind off knitwise.

ASSEMBLY
Fold piece in half matching shoulder markers, and cast-on edge to bound-off edge.
Sew shoulder seam. ■

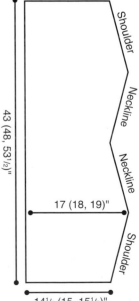

Shoulder
Neckline
Neckline
Shoulder
43 (48, 53½)"
17 (18, 19)"
14½ (15, 15½)"

TRULY TOASTY CLASSIC PONCHO

Design by Kathy Wesley

A classic silhouette and a chunky, roving yarn combine in a poncho that will ward off the chill of any autumn day.

SIZE
Woman's–One size fits most

FINISHED MEASUREMENTS
Each rectangle measures approx 22 x 33 inches

MATERIALS
- Plymouth Yukon Print 35 percent mohair/35 percent wool/30 percent acrylic super bulky weight yarn (60 yds/100g per skein): 10 skeins green print #2001
- Size 13 (9mm) needles or size needed to obtain gauge

GAUGE
10 sts and 13 rows = 4 inches/10cm in Open Ridges pat
   To save time, take time to check gauge.

PATTERN STITCH
Open Ridges
Row 1 (RS): K2, *p1, p2tog, yo, k1, yo, p2tog, p1; rep from * to last 2 sts, k2.
Row 2: K2, purl to last 2 sts, k2.
Row 3: Knit.
Row 4: Rep Row 2.

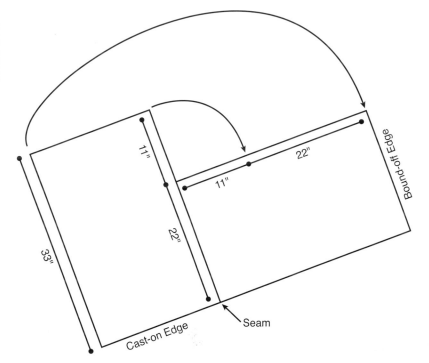

Fig. 1

Rep Rows 1–4 for pat.

PONCHO
Rectangle
Make 2
Cast on 53 sts.
   Knit 2 rows.
   [Rep Rows 1–4 of Open Ridges pat] 28 times.
   Knit 2 rows.

Bind off knitwise on WS.

ASSEMBLY
Block each piece to measure 22 x 33 inches.
   Referring to Fig. 1, sew short end of each piece to longer side of corresponding piece. ■

FASHIONABLE, FRINGED GIRL'S PONCHO

Design by Kathy Wesley

Confetti colors and a swinging fringe will bring a big smile to a little girl's face.

SIZE

Girl's 4 (6, 8)
Instructions are given for smallest size, with larger sizes in parentheses. When only 1 number is given, it applies to all sizes.

MATERIALS

- Plymouth Outback Wool 100 percent virgin wool worsted weight yarn (374 yds/200g per skein): 1 skein rainbow print #995
- Size 11 (8mm) needles or size needed to obtain gauge
- Cable needle

GAUGE

20 sts and 17 rows = 4 inches/10cm in Cable Rib pat
    To save time, take time to check gauge.

SPECIAL ABBREVIATION

CB (Cable Back): Sl next st to cn and hold in back, k1, k1 from cn.

PATTERN STITCH
Cable Rib
Row 1 (RS): K1, p3, *k2, p3; rep from * to last st, k1.
Row 2: K4, *p2, k3; rep from * to last st, k1.
Row 3: K1, p3, *CB, p3; rep from * to last st, k1.
Row 4: Rep Row 2.
    Rep Rows 1–4 for pat.

PATTERN NOTE

Poncho can be worn with either point or straight edge towards front.

PONCHO

Cast on 35 (40, 45) sts.
Set up pat: K4, *p2, k3; rep from * to last st, k1.
    Work even in Cable Rib pat until piece measures 34 (36, 38) inches from beg.
    Bind off.

ASSEMBLY

Place edges side by side and sew 8 (9, 10) inches from lower edge (Fig.1).

FRINGE

Following Fringe instructions on page 170, make single knot fringe. Cut 13-inch strands of yarn.
    Holding 3 strands tog, place knot in every 4th st or row.
    Trim fringe evenly. ■

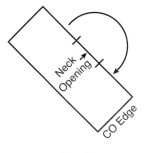

Fig. 1
Sewing Diagram

Supplies

- ☐ Loops & Threads® Braid Yarn (100% acrylic; 100g/100yds)– Rainbow (2 Balls)
- ☐ Crochet Hook: US Size K/10½ (6.5mm) or Size Needed to Obtain Gauge
- ☐ Yarn Needle

Instructions

BACKPACK

Ch 48.

Row 1: Dc in 4th ch from hook, dc in each ch across.
Row 2: Ch 2, dc in each dc across – 46 dc.
Rep Row 2 until Backpack measures 9".
Eyelet Row: Ch1, hdc in same sp, [ch 1, sk next st, hdc in next st] to last st, hdc in last st.
Next Row: Ch 1, sc in each st and ch across. Fasten off.

Sew side seam. Sew bottom seam.

Straps (make 2)

Ch 30.

Row 1: Dc in 4th ch from hook, dc in each ch across.
Row 2: Ch 2, dc in each dc across – 28 dc. Fasten off.

FINISHING

Sew center back seam. Sew bottom seam.

Gauge: 9 sts x 6 rows = 4" in dc; Be sure to check your gauge!

Finished Measurements
Circumference: 20"
Height: 10"

Sew one end of strap to lower back corner, and other end of strap to center at top, just below Eyelet row.
Drawstring: Ch 80, or until drawstring meas 30". Fasten off. Tie each end in a knot. Weave in ends.

Abbreviations:

ch – chain
dc – double crochet
sc - single crochet
hdc - half double crochet
sk - skip
sp - space
rep - repeat
st(s) - stitch(es)

Difficulty: Level 2	Completion Time: 3 Hours	Designed by: Loops and Threads Design Tea

HURRY UP GIFTS

Accessories, as perfect as these, will be appreciated by the recipients. And you'll appreciate how quickly they knit up with big needles.

MAKE ME SMILE ENSEMBLE

Design by Anita Closic

This delightful cloche, scarf, and felted bag will add a touch of whimsy and delight to your day.

SKILL LEVEL
EASY

YARN WEIGHT	YARN WEIGHT	YARN WEIGHT
4 MEDIUM	6 SUPER BULKY	5 BULKY
A	B & D	C

SIZE
Hat circumference: 20 inches
Scarf: 6 x 60 inches
Purse: Approx 10 x 15 after felting

MATERIALS
- Plymouth Galway 100 percent virgin wool worsted weight yarn (210 yds/100g per skein): 1 skein each for hat and purse pink #135 (A)
- Plymouth Parrot 100 percent nylon super bulky weight novelty ribbon yarn (28 yds/50g per ball): 1 ball each for hat and purse pink multi-print #36(B)
- Plymouth Noch Eros 100 percent nylon bulky weight novelty yarn (77 yds/50g per ball): 1 ball for scarf, 2 balls for purse pink variegated #1967 (C)
- Plymouth Rimini Rainbow 60 percent acrylic/40 percent wool super bulky weight yarn (38 yds/ 50g per ball): 2 balls each for hat and scarf, 1 ball for purse rainbow pink #21 (D)
- Size 15 (10mm) needles or size needed to obtain gauge for hat and purse
- Size 19 (15mm) needles
- 6 'Laurel Burch' cat face buttons from Dill Buttons

GAUGE
8 sts = 4 inches/10cm in Rev St st with D and smaller needles
Row gauge is not critical in these projects.

CLOCHE

With smaller needles and B, cast on 40 sts.
Knit 6 rows.
Change to D and knit 1 row.
Work even in rev St st until hat measures 8½ inches from beg, ending with a RS row.

Shape crown
Dec row (WS): K2tog across row. (20 sts)

Purl 1 row.

[Rep dec row] twice. (5 sts)

Cut yarn, leaving a 12-inch end.

Draw yarn through rem sts twice and pull tightly.

Sew back seam.

Turn up cuff at one side of hat only and secure in place with 3 buttons.

SCARF

With larger needles and 1 strand each of D and C held tog, cast on 10 sts.

Pat row: K1, *yo, k2tog, k1; rep from * to last st, k1.

Rep pat row until scarf measures 60 inches.

Bind off loosely.

PURSE

Note: *Two strands of A are held tog for purse.*

With smaller needles and 2 strands of A held tog, cast on 36 sts.

Beg at top of purse and work in garter st throughout in following yarn sequence:

10 rows A

6 rows B

2 rows A

6 rows D

24 rows with A and C

8 rows A (bottom of bag)

24 rows A and C

6 rows D

2 rows A

6 rows B

10 rows A

Bind off loosely.

HANDLE

With 1 strand each of A and C held tog, cast on 4 sts.

*K4, return sts to LH needle; rep from * until handle measures 26 inches.

K4tog, fasten off last st.

TRIM CORDS
Make 2

With 1 strand each of A and C held tog, cast on 3 sts.

*K3, return sts to LH needle; rep from * until trim measures 9 inches.

K3tog, fasten off last st.

ASSEMBLY

Fold purse in half.

With A, sew side seams, forming small gusset at bottom edge.

Sew trim to each side of purse, just above first stripe.

Sew handle to side seams.

FELTING

Place purse in old pillowcase.

Place in washer set on Hot Wash with Cold Rinse.

Checking often, run through cycle until desired amount of felting and size are achieved.

As washers, water temperature and other factors vary, you may need to cycle through more than once, or place in dryer to achieve desired effect.

The key to getting the results you want is to **check the piece often.**

Once the desired size is obtained, stuff the purse with plastic bags to shape it while it air dries.

Sew rem buttons to cord trim. ■

TIE ONE ON–1 STITCH, 4 WAYS

Design by Cindy Polfer

The same elongated stitch combines with different yarns to produce an array of wardrobe accessories.

PATTERN STITCH
Elongated Loop Pattern
Row 1 (RS): K1, *yo twice, k1; rep from * to last st, yo 4 times, k1.
Row 2: Knit, dropping all yo's from needle.
Rows 3 and 4: Knit.
Rep Rows 1–4 for pat.

PATTERN NOTES
Elongated st is made by working a double yo, then dropping extra wraps on the following row. After working Row 2, gently tug stitches to lengthen them.

For **Evening Sparkler Scarf**, 1 strand each of B and C are held tog throughout.

For **Tropicana Scarf**, 1 strand each of D and E are held tog throughout.

For **Berry Pretty Belt**, 1 ball is enough for up to a 60-inch hip circumference.

ELECTRIC BLUE SCARF

SIZE
Approx 4 x 60 inches

MATERIALS
• Plymouth Eros

SKILL LEVEL
■□□□
BEGINNER

YARN WEIGHT
(6)
SUPER BULKY

A

Extreme100 percent nylon super bulky yarn (98 yds/100g per hank): 1 hank electric blue #266 (A)
• Size 15 (10mm) needles or size needed to obtain gauge

GAUGE

12 sts and 8 rows = 4 inches/10cm in Elongated Loop pat
   To save time, take time to check gauge.

SCARF

Cast on 12 sts.
   Knit 4 rows.
   Work even in Elongated Loop pat until scarf measures approx 59 inches, ending with Row 4 of pat.
   Knit 2 rows.
   Bind off knitwise.

EVENING SPARKLER SCARF

SIZE

Approx 3½ x 58 inches

SKILL LEVEL
BEGINNER

YARN WEIGHT
4 MEDIUM

MATERIALS

• Plymouth 24K 82 percent nylon/18 percent lamé worsted weight yarn (187 yds/50g per ball): 1 ball multi-colored print #468 (B)
• Plymouth Electra 100 percent nylon worsted weight eyelash yarn (125 yds/50g per ball): 1 ball gray tones #15 (C)
• Size 11 (8mm) needles or size needed to obtain gauge

B & C

GAUGE

12 sts and 8 rows = 3½ inches in Elongated Loop pat
   To save time, take time to check gauge.

SCARF

With 1 strand each of B & C held tog, cast on 12 sts.
   Knit 4 rows.
   Work even in Elongated Loop pat until scarf measures approx 58 inches, ending with Row 4 of pat.
   Knit 2 rows.
   Bind off knitwise.

TROPICANA SCARF

SIZE

Approx 3½ x 48 inches, excluding fringe

SKILL LEVEL
BEGINNER

YARN WEIGHT
4 MEDIUM

D

MATERIALS

- Plymouth Eros 100 percent nylon worsted weight novelty yarn (165 yds/50g per ball): 1 turquoise multi #4796 (D)
- Plymouth Colorlash 100 percent polyester eyelash carry-along yarn (220 yds/50g per ball): 1 lime green #1 (E)
- Size 11 (8mm) needles or size needed to obtain gauge
- Size G/6 (4mm) crochet hook

GAUGE

12 sts and 8 rows = 3½ inches in Elongated Loop pat.

To save time, take time to check gauge.

SCARF

With 1 strand each of D & E held tog, cast on 12 sts.

Knit 4 rows.

Work even in Elongated Loop pat until scarf measures approx 48 inches, ending with Row 4 of pat.

Knit 2 rows.

Bind off knitwise. Cut yarn leaving a 6-inch end.

FRINGE

Following Fringe instructions on page 170, make single knot fringe. Cut 12-inch strands each of D & E.

Holding 1 strand of each yarn tog, place knot in each st along cast-on edge,.

Rep along bound-off edge.

Trim fringe even.

BERRY PRETTY BELT

SIZE

Approx 2¼ inches x desired waist/hip measurement + 12 inches, excluding fringe

SKILL LEVEL
■□□□
BEGINNER

YARN WEIGHT
5
BULKY

F

MATERIALS

- Plymouth Noch Eros 100 percent nylon bulky weight novelty yarn (77 yds/50g per ball): 1 ball pink multi #1967 (F)
- Size 11 (8mm) needles or size needed to obtain gauge
- Size G/6 (4mm) crochet hook

GAUGE

14 sts and 8 rows = 4 inches/ 10cm in Elongated Loop pat

To save time, take time to check gauge.

BELT

Cast on 8 sts.

Knit 4 rows.

Work even in Elongated Loop pat until belt measures desired waist/hip length plus 12 inches, ending with Row 4 of pat.

Knit 2 rows.

Bind off knitwise. Cut yarn leaving a 6-inch end.

FRINGE

Following Fringe instructions on page 170, make single knot fringe. Cut 12-inch strands of yarn. Using 1 strand for each knot, place a knot in each st along cast-on edge.

Rep along bound-off edge.

Trim fringe even. ■

MERRIMENT MITTENS FOR ONE & ALL

Design by Colleen Smitherman

Knit these colorful mittens on two circular needles instead of double points. A doubled strand of yarn makes it a quick and enjoyable project.

SIZE
Child small (child medium, child large/ adult small, adult medium, adult large) Instructions are given for smallest size, with larger sizes in parentheses. When only 1 number is given, it applies to all sizes.

SKILL LEVEL
■■■□
INTERMEDIATE

YARN WEIGHT
4
MEDIUM
MC

YARN WEIGHT
6
SUPER BULKY
CC

FINISHED MEASUREMENTS
Length: 7½ (8½, 9½, 10¼, 11) inches
Width: 3 (3½, 3¾, 3¾, 4¼) inches

MATERIALS
• Plymouth Galway 100 percent wool worsted weight yarn (210 yds/100g per skein): 1 skein Adult: bright pink #125, Child: sage green #130 (MC)

• Plymouth Rimini Rainbow 60 percent acrylic/40 percent wool super bulky weight yarn (38 yds/50g per ball): 1 ball rainbow white #10 (CC)
• (2) Size 12 (8.5mm) 16-inch circular needles or size needed to obtain gauge
• Small amount scrap yarn

GAUGE
13 sts and 20 rows = 4 inches/ 10cm in St st with 2 strands of MC held tog
To save time, take time to check gauge.

PATTERN NOTES
Body of mitten is knit first in the round with sts divided between 2 circular needles. (See Working on Two Circular Needles, page 142.)
Cuff sts are picked up at the cast-on edge, then worked back and forth in garter stitch.

RIGHT MITTEN
With 2 strands of MC held tog, cast on 22 (24, 26, 26, 28) sts.
Sl half of sts to 2nd needle and begin knitting in the round being careful not to twist sts when joining.

Workeven in St st until mitten measures 1¾ (2¼, 2½, 2 ¾, 3) inches from beg.

Beg thumb opening

Next rnd: K1 MC, drop MC, with scrap yarn k4 (4, 5, 5, 6) sts, drop scrap yarn, sl sts just worked with scrap yarn back to LH needle.

With MC, knit across scrap yarn sts and to end of rnd.

Work even until mitten measures 3¼ (3¾, 4¼, 4½, 5) inches above thumb opening.

Shape top

Dec rnd: *K1, k2tog, knit to last 3 sts, ssk, k1; rep from * on 2nd needle. (9, 10, 11, 11, 12 sts on each needle)

Rep dec rnd until 5 (6, 5, 5, 6) sts remain on each needle.

Cut yarn, leaving a 12-inch end.

Weave top of mitten tog, using Kitchener st as shown on page 170.

THUMB

Remove scrap yarn and place resulting sts on each side of opening on 2 needles, having 4 (4, 5, 5, 6) sts on each needle.

Pick up 1 additional st at each end of opening and place on needle. (10, 10, 12, 12, 14 sts)

Join 2 strands of MC, leaving a 9-inch end.

Work even in St st until thumb measures 1½ (2¼, 2¼, 2¼, 2¾) inches.

Shape thumb tip

For Child small and child medium sizes only

Next Row: [K2tog] 5 times. (5 sts)

For Child large/adult small, adult medium, and adult large sizes only

Next Row: *K1, k2tog, knit to last 3 sts, ssk, k1; rep from * on second needle. (8, 8, 10)

For All sizes

Cut yarn leaving an 8-inch end.

Draw yarn through rem 5 (5, 8, 8, 10) sts twice and pull tightly.

At base of thumb, use each yarn tail to tighten any gaps in sts.

CUFF

With RS facing and 1 strand of CC, pick up and knit 8 (9, 10, 10, 11) sts across palm of mitten on first needle

and 8 (9, 10, 10, 11) sts across back of mitten on 2nd needle.

Do not join; work in rows.

Knit 5 (5, 5, 8, 8) rows.

Bind off knitwise.

Sew sides of cuff tog.

LEFT MITTEN

Work as for right mitten until piece measures 1¾ (2¼, 2½, 2¾, 3) inches from beg.

Beg thumb opening

Next rnd: With first needle, k 6 (7, 7, 7, 7) sts with MC, drop MC, k4 (4, 5, 5, 6) sts with scrap yarn, drop scrap yarn, sl 4 (4, 5, 5, 6) sts back to LH needle.

With MC, complete as for right mitten. ■

Working on two circular needles

If you have avoided knitting in the round because of the challenge of using double-pointed needles, you will love this technique. To begin, divide sts between 2 circular needles. You will knit sts on each needle only with that needle.

For each round:

1. Slide sts not in work to center of free needle, where they will be secure.

2. Holding working needle in left hand, slide sts to the tip of needle so they are in normal working position. With right hand, bring free end of same needle to working position. Knit all the sts on this needle.

3. Rep Steps 1–2 for 2nd needle.

Cast-on tail will serve as a marker for beg/end of rnd.

WARM PLEASURES HAT, WRISTERS & SCARF

Designs by Diane Zangl

This fashionable set is suitable for all—from middle school to college students to the teachers and parents who educate them.

SIZE
One size fits most adults

SKILL LEVEL
■■□□
EASY

YARN WEIGHT
4
MEDIUM
A

YARN WEIGHT
5
BULKY
B

**FINISHED
MEASUREMENTS
Beret circumference:**
20 inches
Wristers: 9 inches
long

Scarf: Approx 7 x 50 inches

MATERIALS
- Plymouth Outback Wool 100 percent virgin wool worsted weight yarn (374 yds/200g per hank): 1 hank midnight blues #996 (A)
- Plymouth Outback Mohair 70 percent mohair/26 percent wool/4 percent nylon bulky weight yarn (220 yds/100g per hank): 1 hank purple/blue variegated #896 (B)
- Size 8 (5mm) 16-inch circular and double-pointed needles
- Size 10½ (6.5mm) 16-inch circular and double-pointed needles or size needed to obtain gauge
- Stitch markers

GAUGE
12 sts and 17 rows = 4 inches/ 10cm in St st with A and B held tog
11 sts and 17 rows = 4 inches/ 10cm in Openwork pat with A and B held tog
To save time, take time to check gauge.

PATTERN STITCH
Openwork
Row 1 (RS): Sl 1 knitwise wyib, *yo, k2tog; rep from * across.
Row 2: Sl 1 purlwise wyif, purl to end of row.
Rep Rows 1 and 2 for pat.

PATTERN NOTES
Yarn amounts given are sufficient for all three pieces.

One strand each of A and B are held tog for MC.

Two strands each of A are held tog for CC.

SCARF

With MC and larger circular needle, cast on 19 sts.

Purl 1 row.

Work even in Openwork pat until scarf measures 50 inches, ending with a WS row.

Bind off knitwise.

BERET

With CC and smaller circular needle,

cast on 74 sts. Join without twisting, pm between first and last st.

Ribbing rnd: *K1-tbl, p1; rep from * around.

[Rep Ribbing rnd] 6 times more. Change to MC and larger needles. Knit 1 rnd, inc 3 sts evenly. (77 sts)

Work even in St st until beret measures 5 inches from beg.

Place markers after every 11th st. (7 markers in all)

Shape crown

Dec rnd: [Knit to 2 sts before marker, k2tog] 7 times.

Knit 1 rnd.

Rep last 2 rnds until 7 sts rem, changing to dpn when necessary.

Top Loop

Next rnd: K1, [k2tog] 3 times. (4 sts)

Place all 4 sts on 1 dpn. Using 2nd dpn, *k4, sl sts back on LH needle; rep from * until lp measures 1½ inches.

Dec row: [K2tog] twice, sl sts back on LH needle, k2tog.

Fasten off last st. Cut yarn, leaving an 8-inch end.

Fold lp in half, and wrap yarn end around base of lp 2 or 3 times. Thread end into needle and draw end to inside. Fasten tightly.

Dampen beret and stretch over a dinner plate. Let dry thoroughly.

WRISTERS

Make 2

Beg at fingers with smaller dpn and CC, cast on 30 sts. Join without twisting, pm between first and last st.

Work even in Ribbing rnd as for Beret for 5 rnds.

Change to larger needles and MC.

Knit 1 rnd, dec 4 sts evenly. (26 sts)

Knit 2 rnds. Remove marker and work in rows from this point.

Thumb opening

Row 1 (RS): Sl 1 knitwise wyib, p1, knit to last 2 sts, p1, k1.

Row 2: Sl 1 purlwise wyif, k1, purl to last 2 sts, k1, p1.

[Rep Rows 1–2] 3 times more. Replace marker, join and work in rnds from this point.

Knit 2 rnds, inc 1 st each side of marker on last rnd. (28 sts)

Work even until wrister measures 8 inches from beg.

Change to CC and smaller needles.

[Rep Ribbing rnd] 5 times. Bind off loosely in rib. ■

FOR YOU & YOUR PAMPERED POOCH

Design by Gayle Bunn

You and Fido can flaunt your style and stay warm at the same time in matching walking gear.

SIZE

Hat and Mittens: One size fits most

Dog coat: Extra-small (small, medium, large) Instructions are given for smallest size, with larger sizes in parentheses. When only 1 number is given, it applies to all sizes.

FINISHED MEASUREMENTS
MITTEN
Length: 11 inches

DOG COAT
Chest: 11 (13½, 16, 20) inches
Length: 11 (13, 16, 21) inches

MATERIALS
- Plymouth Yukon 35 percent mohair/35 percent wool/30 percent acrylic super bulky weight yarn (59 yds/100g per skein): **Hat & mittens:** 3 skeins **Dog coat:** 1 skein pink #959 (MC)
- Plymouth Flash 100% nylon medium weight eyelash yarn (190 yds/50g per ball): 1 ball white #900 (A)
- Plymouth Baby Alpaca Brush 80 percent baby alpaca/20 percent acrylic bulky weight yarn (110 yds/50g per ball): 1 ball soft white #1000 (B)
- Size 11 (8mm) straight and double-pointed needles or size needed to obtain gauge
- Size 15 (10mm) straight and 24-inch circular needles or size needed to obtain gauge
- Cable needle
- Stitch holders
- Stitch markers

GAUGE
Hat and Dog Coat:
6 sts and 12 rows = 4 inches/10cm in St st with MC and larger needles
Mittens:
7 sts and 14 rows = 4 inches/10cm in St st with MC and smaller needles
   To save time, take time to check gauge.

SPECIAL ABBREVIATIONS
C4B (Cable 4 Back): Sl next 2 sts to cn and hold in back, k2, k2 from cn.
C4F (Cable 4 Front): Sl next 2 sts to cn and hold in front, k2, k2 from cn.

PATTERN STITCH
Cable Panel
Row 1 (RS): P1, k8, p1.
Row 2 and all WS rows: K1, p8, k1.
Row 3: P1, C4B, C4F, p1.
Rows 5 and 7: Rep Row 1.
Row 8: Rep Row 2.
   Rep Rows 1–8 for pat.

PATTERN NOTES
Two strands of A and 1 strand of B are held tog for trim. This will be referred to as CC.
   Mittens are worked back and

forth in rows with a seam at outside of hand.

HAT

With MC and larger needles, cast on 39 sts.

Row 1 (RS): K1, *p1, k1; rep from * across.

Row 2: P1, *k1, p1; rep from * across.

Rep Rows 1–2 until hat measures 4 inches, ending with a RS row.

Next row (WS): Rib 15, [inc 1 st in next st, rib 3] twice, inc 1 st in next st, rib to end of row. (42 sts)

Set up pat

Row 1 (RS): Work across first 6 sts and sl to holder, k10, pm, work Row 1 of Cable Panel, pm, k10, place rem 6 sts on holder.

Row 2: P10, work Row 2 of Cable Panel, p10.

Keeping sts between markers in established Cable Panel and rem sts in St st, work even until hat measures 11 inches from beg, ending with a WS row.

Shape top

Row 1: Work 21 sts (1 st past marker), turn, leaving rem sts unworked.

Row 2: Sl 1 purlwise, work 10 Cable Panel sts, p2tog, turn, leave rem sts unworked.

Row 3: Sl 1 purlwise, work 10 Cable Panel sts, ssk, turn, leave rem sts unworked.

Rep Rows 2 and 3 until all sts on either side have been worked.

Place rem 12 sts on holder.

FRONT EDGING

With RS facing and MC, work in established rib pat across 6 sts of first holder, pick up and knit 15 sts along side of hat, knit 12 sts from top st holder dec 1 st at center, pick up and knit 16 sts down other side of hat, work in established rib pat across 6 sts of rem st holder. (55 sts)

Work even in k1, p1 rib for 3 rows.

Cut MC, change to CC.

Knit 2 rows; purl 1 row.

Loosely bind off knitwise on WS.

Sew neckband seam, including face trim.

MITTENS

LEFT MITTEN

With CC and smaller needles, cast on 19 sts loosely.

Row 1 (RS): Purl.

Row 2: Knit.

Row 3: Purl.

Change to MC.

Next row: P3, [inc 1 st in next st, p3] twice, inc 1 st in next st, purl to end of row. (22 sts)

Set up pat

Row 1 (RS): K10, pm, work Row 1 of Cable Panel, pm, k2.

Row 2: P2, work Row 2 of Cable Panel, p10.

Keeping sts between markers in established Cable Panel and rem sts in St st, work even until mitten measures 2½ inches from beg, ending with a WS row.

Beg thumb gusset

Row 1: K7, inc 1 st in each of next 2 sts, work pat to end.

Work 3 rows even.

Row 5: K7, inc 1 st in next st, k2, inc 1 st in next st, work to end.

Work 3 rows even.

Row 9: K7, inc 1 st in next st, k4, inc 1 st in next st, work to end.

Work 1 row even.

Beg thumb

Row 1: K15, turn, leave rem sts unworked.

Row 2: Cast on 1 st, p7, turn, leave rem sts unworked.

Row 3: Cast on 1 st, k8. (9 sts) Work 3 rows even.

Shape top of thumb

Dec Row 1: [K1, k2tog] 3 times. (6 sts)

Purl 1 row.

Dec Row 2: [K2tog] 3 times. (3 sts)

Cut yarn, leaving an 8-inch end.

Draw yarn through rem sts twice and pull tightly.

Sew thumb seam.

Hand

With RS facing, rejoin yarn to sts from RH needle, pick up and knit 2 sts at base of thumb, work in established pat to end of row.

Next row: Work in established pat, purling tog 2 sts picked up at base of thumb. (22 sts.)

Work even until mitten measures 10 inches from beg, ending with a WS row.

Shape top

Dec Row 1: [K1, k2tog] 7 times, k1. (15 sts)

Purl 1 row.

Dec Row 2: [K2tog] 7 times, k1 (8 sts)

Cut yarn leaving a long end.

Draw yarn through rem sts twice and pull tightly.

Sew side seam.

RIGHT MITTEN

With CC and smaller needles, cast on 19 sts loosely.

Row 1 (RS): Purl.

Row 2: Knit.

Row 3: Purl.

Change to MC.

Next row: P10, [inc 1 st in next st, p3] twice, inc 1 st in next st, purl to end of row. (22 sts)

Set up pat

Row 1 (RS): K2, pm, work Row 1 of Cable Panel, pm, k10.

Row 2: P10, work Row 2 of Cable Panel, p2.

Keeping sts between markers in established Cable Panel and rem sts in St st, work even until mitten measures 2½ inches from beg, ending with a WS row.

Beg thumb gusset

Row 1: Work in established pat across 12 sts, inc 1 st in each of

next 2 sts, knit to end of row.

Complete thumb and remainder of mitten as for left mitten.

DOG COAT

Beg at collar with CC and larger needles, loosely cast on 18 (22, 26, 32) sts.

Row 1 (RS): Purl.

Row 2: Knit.

Row 3: Purl.

Change to MC.

Inc row: P6 (8, 10, 13), [inc 1 st in next st, p3] twice, purl to end of row. (20, 24, 28, 34 sts)

Set up pat

Row 1 (RS): K5 (7, 9, 12), pm, work Row 1 of Cable Panel, pm, K5 (7, 9, 12).

Row 2: P5 (7, 9, 12), work Row 2 of Cable Panel, P5 (6, 9, 12).

Keeping sts between markers in established Cable Panel and rem sts in St st, inc 1 st each end every RS row 4 (5, 6, 7) times. (28, 34, 40, 48 sts)

Work even until coat measures 3½ (4, 6, 8) inches above collar, ending with a WS row.

Leg openings

Row 1: K3 (5, 7, 9), bind off 3 (4, 4, 5) sts, work in pat across 16 (16, 18, 20) sts, bind off 3 (4, 4, 5) sts, k3 (5, 7, 9).

Note: All Leg Sections are worked *at the same time* using a separate ball of yarn for each section.

Beg with a WS row, work even for 3 (5, 5, 7) rows.

Next row (RS): K3 (5, 7, 9), cast on 3 (4, 4, 5) sts, work in pat across 16 (16, 18, 20) sts, cast on 3 (4, 4, 5) sts, K3 (5, 7, 9). (28, 34, 40, 48 sts)

Work even in established pat until coat measures 6 (8, 11, 16) inches above collar, ending with a WS row.

Back shaping

Bind off 3 (4, 5, 7) sts at beg of next 2 rows. (22 26, 30, 34) sts.

Dec row: Ssk, work in pat to last 2 sts, k2tog.

Work 1 row even.

[Rep last 2 rows] 9 (10, 11, 13) times. (10, 14, 18, 22 sts)

Work even until back measures 5 inches above bound-off back sts.

Place rem sts on holder; cut MC.

BACK EDGING

With RS facing, using larger circular needle and MC, pick up and knit 11 (14, 19, 25) sts along bound-off and shaped back edge, work across 10 (14, 18, 22) sts from holder dec 2 sts evenly across, pick up and knit 11 (14, 19, 25) sts along opposite side of back. (30, 40, 54, 70 sts)

Change to CC.

Knit 1 row; purl 1 row.

Loosely bind off knitwise on WS.

Sew collar and body seam.

LEGS

With dpn and MC, pick up and knit 18 (20, 20, 24) sts around leg opening.

Divide sts so there are 6 (8, 8, 8) sts on first needle and 6 (6, 6, 8) sts each on 2nd and 3rd needles.

Join, place marker between first and last st.

Work even in k1, p1 ribbing for 3 rnds.

Bind off in rib. ∎

PAINT THE TOWN

Design by Gayle Bunn

Vests always impart a distinctive touch to any ensemble. With the addition of a smart tote, you'll be ready to step out in style.

SIZE

Woman's small (medium, large, extra-large) Instructions are given for smallest size, with larger sizes in parentheses. When only 1 number is given, it applies to all sizes

SKILL LEVEL
EASY

YARN WEIGHT
6 SUPER BULKY
MC

YARN WEIGHT
5 BULKY
CC

FINISHED MEASUREMENTS
VEST
Chest: 34, (36, 38, 40) inches
Length: 18 (18½, 19½, 20) inches
TOTE
Approx 8 inches at base x 10 inches at top x 7½ inches high

MATERIALS

- Plymouth Encore Mega 75 percent acrylic/25 percent wool (64 yds/100g per skein) 3 (3, 4, 5) skeins for vest; 2 skeins for tote ecru #256 (MC)
- Plymouth Furlauro 100 percent nylon bulky weight eyelash yarn (82 yds/50g per ball): 3 (3, 4, 4) balls for vest; 2 balls for tote multi-colored #816 (CC)
- Size 15 (10mm) straight and 36-inch circular needles or size needed to obtain gauge
- Size J/13 (9mm) crochet hook
- Stitch markers

GAUGE

7 sts and 12 rows = 4 inches/10cm in St st with 1 strand each yarn held tog

To save time, take time to check gauge.

VEST

BACK

With 1 strand of each yarn held tog, cast on 25 (27, 29, 31) sts.

Beg with a knit row, work 4 rows in St st.

Inc 1 st each end of next and following 19th row. (29, 31, 33, 35 sts)

Work even in St st until back measures 10½ (10½, 11, 11) inches ending with a WS row.

Shape armholes
Bind off 3 sts beg of next 2 rows. (23, 25, 27, 29 sts)

[Dec 1 st each end of every RS row] twice. (19, 21, 23, 25 sts)

Work even until armhole measures 6½ (7, 7½, 8) inches above bound-off underarm sts, ending with a WS row.

Shape neck
Next row (RS): K4 (5, 5, 6), join 2nd ball of yarn and bind off next 11 (11, 13, 13) sts, k4 (5, 5, 6).

Working both sides of neck at

same time with separate balls of yarn, work 3 rows even.

Bind off.

LEFT FRONT

With 1 strand of each yarn held tog, cast on 6 (7, 8, 9) sts.

Knit 1 row.

[Inc 1 st at front edge every row] 3 times. (9, 10, 11, 12 sts)

Inc 1 st at side edge on next and following 19th row, *at the same time* continue to [inc 1 st at front edge every row] 4 times. (15, 16, 17, 18 sts)

Work even until front measures same as for back to underarm, ending with a WS row.

Shape armhole and front edge
Next row (RS): Bind off 3 sts, knit to last 2 sts, k2tog at front edge.

Purl 1 row.

[Dec 1 st each at arm edge on every RS row] twice, *at the same time* [dec 1 st at front edge every 4th row] 5 (5, 6, 6) times more. (4, 5, 5, 6 sts)

Work even until armhole measures same as for back above bound-off underarm sts, ending with a WS row.

Bind off.

RIGHT FRONT

With 1 strand of each yarn held tog, cast on 6 (7, 8, 9) sts.

Knit 1 row.

[Inc 1 st at front edge every row] 3 times. (9, 10, 11, 12 sts)

Inc 1 st at side edge on next and following 19th row, *at the same time* continue to [inc 1 st at front edge every row] 4 times. (15, 16, 17, 18 sts)

Work even until front measures same as for back to underarm, ending with a RS row.

Shape armhole and front edge
Next row (WS): Bind off 3 sts, purl to end of row.

[Dec 1 st each at arm edge on every RS row] twice, *at the same time* [dec 1 st at front edge every 4th row] 5 (5, 6, 6) times more. (4, 5, 5, 6 sts)

Work even until armhole measures same as for back above bound-off underarm sts, ending with a WS row.

Bind off.

Sew shoulder seams.

ARMHOLE EDGING

With RS facing and 1 strand of each yarn held tog, pick up and knit 43 (46, 49, 52) sts evenly around armhole.

Bind off knitwise on WS.

Sew side seams.

BODY EDGING

Beg at left side seam with 2 strands of CC held tog and circular needle, pick up and knit 65 (69, 73, 77) sts along lower and left front edge to shoulder, 4 sts along left back neck edge, 13 (13, 15, 15) sts across back neck, 4 sts along right back neck edge, 65 (69, 73, 77) sts along right front and lower edge to side seam and 29 (31, 33, 35) sts across lower back. (180, 190, 202, 212 sts)

Join, place marker between first and last st. Turn work so WS is facing; knit 3 rnds.

Loosely bind off knitwise.

TIES

Note: *If not familiar with crochet chain refer to page 173.*

Holding 1 strand of each yarn tog, join yarn with sl st at beg of neck shaping.

With crochet hook, make a chain 9 inches long.

Fasten off.

Rep for opposite side.

PURSE

BODY
Make 2

With 1 strand of each yarn held tog, cast on 15 sts.

Work 2 rows in St st.

Inc 1 st each end of next and following 11th row. (19 sts)

Work even in St st until purse measures 6 inches, ending with a WS row.

Cut MC; with 2 strands of A held tog, knit 2 rows.

Work in rev St st for 3 rows.

Pm at each end of last row for fold line.

Cut 1 strand of CC; join MC.

With 1 strand of each yarn held tog and beg with a knit row, work even in St st for 6 rows.

Bind off.

HANDLES
Make 2

With 1 strand of each yarn held tog, cast on 4 sts.

Row 1 (RS): [K1, p1] twice.

Row 2: [P1, k1] twice.

Rep last 2 rows until handle measures 14 inches ending with a WS row.

Bind off in pat.

ASSEMBLY

Sew sides and lower edge of purse pieces tog.

Turn top edge to inside along fold line and sew bound-off edge in place.

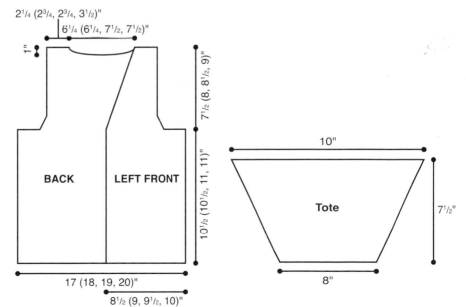

Sew ends of each handle to WS 1 inch from fold line and 2 inches in from each side edge. ■

GOOD TIMES HAT & SCARF

Design by Celeste Pinheiro

Bright ribbon yarn adds a colorful touch to a soft and warm mohair set.

SIZE
Adult–One size fits most

SKILL LEVEL
INTERMEDIATE

YARN WEIGHT
4
MEDIUM

YARN WEIGHT
5
BULKY

FINISHED MEASUREMENTS
Scarf: 4½ x 80 inches
Hat circumference: 23 inches

MATERIALS
- Plymouth Outback Mohair 70 percent mohair/26 percent wool/4 percent nylon bulky weight yarn (218 yds/100g per skein): 2 skeins Mardi Gras #895 (MC)
- Plymouth Parrot 100 percent nylon super bulky weight ribbon yarn (28 yds/50g per ball): 1 ball pink multi-print #36 (CC)
- Size 11 (8mm) needles or size needed to obtain gauge
- Size 15 (10mm) needles or size needed to obtain gauge

GAUGE
12 sts and 24 rows = 4 inches/10cm in garter st with single strand of MC and smaller needles
10 sts and 16 rows = 4 inches/10cm in St st with 2 strands of MC held tog and smaller needles
To save time, take time to check gauge.

SCARF

With larger needles, cast on 245 sts.
Change to smaller needles.
Rows 1–3: Knit.
Row 4: *K2tog, yo; rep from * to last st, k1.
Rows 5–9: Knit.
Rows 10–15: Rep Rows 4–9.
Row 16: Rep Row 4.
Rows 17–19: Knit.
Change to larger needle.
Bind off loosely.

ASSEMBLY
Cut 3 strands CC, each 110 inches long.
Weave 1 strand through each eyelet row; adjust trailing ends evenly.
Cut 6 strands of CC, each 30 inches long.
Thread 1 strand through hole at end of each eyelet row, and tie into knot with threaded strand.
Trim fringe to desired length.

HAT

Beg at brim with MC and smaller needles, cast on 79 sts.
Knit 3 rows.

Next row (RS): *K2tog, yo; rep from * to last st, k1.
Knit 5 rows.
[Rep last 6 rows] once.
Purl 1 row.

Begin crown
Join 2nd strand of MC. Working with 2 strands of MC held tog, knit 1 row, dec 23 sts evenly spaced. (56 sts)
Beg with a purl row, work even in St st until hat measures 9 inches from beg, ending with a WS row.

Shape crown
Dec row (RS): *K5, k2tog; rep from * across. (48 sts)
Purl 1 row.
2nd Dec Row: *K4, k2tog; rep from * across. (40 sts)
Purl 1 row.
3rd Dec Row: *K3, k2tog; rep from * across. (32 sts)
Continue to dec every other row as established until 8 sts rem.
Cut yarn, leaving a 20-inch end.
Draw yarn through rem sts twice and pull tightly.
Sew back seam.

TRIM
Cut 2 strands CC, each 26 inches long.
Weave 1 strand through each Eyelet Row on brim.
Tie ends in knot.
Fold up brim. ■

For more project ideas
visit michaels.com

Project Sheet #34489
POG #s- 4/511/P 4/711/P
6/7/2013- 6/7/2014

Supplies

- ☐ Loops & Threads® Glitz™ (1.25 oz. /35 ga.) Yarn – Red (1 Ball)
- ☐ Scissors

Tip

One ball makes several cowls.

Instructions

Step 1 Cut a length of yarn approximately 88" in length.

Step 2 Starting at one end, insert hand into yarn-tube, stretching out the yarn. Working towards the other end, continue to stretch out the yarn using one hand to gather the edges.

Step 3 When the full length of yarn has been stretched (forming a ring), grasp both sides of the ring and pull your hands apart to form and secure the cowl.

| **Difficulty: Level 2** | **Completion Time: 5 Minutes** | **Designed by: Loops & Threads Design Team** |

Where Creativity Happens

No Knit
No Crochet
Make this scarf
in minutes
5 easy steps

Imagine Scarf
Lion Brand® Imagine®

34727

Tip

For a fun, 'fuller' look, repeat Steps 1-5. This variation will create a shorter Scarf.

Supplies

☐ LION BRAND® IMAGINE® (Art. #515)
#309 Strawberry Fields 1 ball
or colors of your choice

Instructions
Gauge

EXACT GAUGE IS NOT ESSENTIAL TO THIS PROJECT.

Scarf

This yarn is a tube!

1. Slide your hand into one end of the yarn tube.

2. Slide the yarn up and gather the tube onto your arm until your hand emerges from the other end.

3. With your other hand, grab the uppermost edge of the yarn tube and gently pull it down over itself.

4. Continue pulling until both ends of the tube meet.

5. Holding both ends together, slide the tube off your arm. You now have a double layer of the yarn. Suggestion: Knot the ends to keep the layers in place.

| Difficulty: Beginner | Completion Time: 1 hr or less | Designed by: Lion Brand® |

Michaels
Where Creativity Happens®

FLUFF WITH STYLE

Design by Cindy Polfer

Tapered ends and a slit opening make a scarf that's a breeze to wear.

SIZE
Approx 3½ x 30 inches

SKILL LEVEL
EASY

YARN WEIGHT
4
MEDIUM

MATERIALS
• Plymouth Flash 100 percent nylon worsted weight eyelash yarn (71 yds/ 50g per ball): 2 balls light peach #992
• Size 11 (8mm) needles or size needed to obtain gauge
• Stitch holders

GAUGE
16 sts and 16 rows = 3½ inches in garter st with 2 strands of yarn held tog

To save time, take time to check gauge.

PATTERN NOTES
Scarf is worked with 2 strands of yarn held tog throughout.

Inc is made by knitting in front and back of st.

Dec is made by working k2tog. Yarn is brushed after knitting to increase its fluffiness.

SCARF
With 2 strands of yarn held tog, cast on 2 sts.

Shape end
Row 1: Knit in front and back of each st. (4 sts)

Row 2: [Inc, k1] twice. (6 sts)

Row 3: Inc, knit to last 2 sts, inc, k1. (8 sts)

Rows 4 and 5: Rep Row 3. (12 sts)

Row 6: Knit.

Row 7: Rep Row 3. (14 sts)

Row 8: Knit.

Row 9: Rep Row 3. (16 sts)

Work even for 7 rows.

Divide for slit
Knit 8 sts, place rem sts on holder.

Knit 6 rows, ending at center of scarf.

Cut yarn and slip these sts to 2nd holder.

Sl sts from first holder to needle.

Join yarn at slit and knit 8 rows, ending at slit.

Close slit
Sl sts from holder to LH needle and knit across them.

Work even in garter st until 4 yds of yarn remain.

Shape end
Row 1: K2tog, knit to last 2 sts, k2tog. (14 sts)

Rows 2 and 4: Knit.

Rows 3, 5, 6, 7, 8, and 9: Rep Row 1. (2 sts)

Bind off. ■

CLAUDIA'S FELTED PURSE WITH SCARF

Design by Ellen Edwards Drechsler

Take advantage of all the great novelty yarns available by creating a felted purse with a decorative scarf to coordinate with all your outfits

SKILL LEVEL
INTERMEDIATE

YARN WEIGHT **4** MEDIUM — MC

YARN WEIGHT **6** SUPER BULKY — A

YARN WEIGHT **5** BULKY — B

SIZE
Approx 29 inches around x 8 inches high, after felting

MATERIALS
- Plymouth Galway 100 percent virgin wool worsted weight yarn (210 yds/100g per skein): 4 skeins pink #135 **or** teal #131 (MC)
- Plymouth Jungle 100 percent nylon super bulky weight novelty ribbon yarn (61 yds/50g per ball): **For pink purse:** 1 ball pink/orange print #2 (A)
- Plymouth Odyssey Glitz 60 percent nylon/37 percent wool/3 percent lamé bulky weight novelty yarn (66 yds/50g per ball): **For teal purse:** 1 ball rainbow multi #916 (B)
- Size 11 (8mm) 32-inch circular and 2 double-pointed needles or size needed to obtain gauge
- Size 15 (10mm) needles

- Size I/9 (5.5mm) crochet hook (optional)
- Stitch holders
- Stitch markers

GAUGE
11 sts = 4 inches/10cm in St st with smaller needles and 2 strands of MC held tog

Row gauge is not critical for this project.

PATTERN NOTE
Two strands of MC are held tog for entire purse.

PURSE

BOTTOM
With smaller circular needle and 2 strands of MC held tog, cast on 20 sts.
Knit 40 rows

Beg sides
With 20 sts on RH needle, pick up and knit 40 sts along side edge, 20 sts across cast-on sts, and 40 sts along rem side edge, pm between first and last st. (120 sts)

Join. Work in St st until sides measure 10 inches above picked-up sts.

Beg scarf openings
K10, turn. Work in St st on these 10 sts only for 5 more rows. Cut yarn and place sts on holder.

Rejoin yarn at next st, bind off 5 sts, k10, turn. Work in St st on these 10 sts only for 5 more rows. Cut yarn and place sts on holder.

Rep from * to * until all sts have been worked. Do not cut yarn on last section.

Next rnd: *Knit across section, cast on 5 sts; rep from * around. (120 sts)

Work even in St st for 1½ inches above cast-on sts of openings.

Dec rnd: *K4, k2tog; rep from * around. (100 sts)

Beg I-cord handles
Next rnd: K8, bind off next 42 sts, k8 and place on holder, knit to end of rnd.

Sl next 8 sts to dpn.

*K8, slide sts to opposite end of needle, bring yarn around back to first st and rep from * until handle is 29 inches long.

If necessary, use crochet hook to latch up wide 'ladder' where yarn was carried across back of handle.

Sew these 8 sts to 8 sts on

holder, using Kitchener method shown on page 170.

Weave in ends.

SCARF

With matching yarn A or B and larger needles, cast on 8 sts.

Work even in garter st until scarf measures 48 inches.

Bind off.

FELTING

Place purse in old pillowcase.

Place in washer set on Hot Wash with Cold Rinse.

Checking often, run through cycle until desired amount of felting and size are achieved.

As washers, water temperature and other factors vary, you may need to cycle through more than once, or place in dryer to achieve desired effect.

The key to getting the results you want is to **check the piece often.**

Once the desired size is obtained, stuff the purse with plastic bags to shape it while it air dries.

ASSEMBLY

Weave scarf through openings, beg and ending center of bag between handles.

Tie ends in a bow or decorative knot. ■

EDITH'S FELTED DRAWSTRING BAG

Design by Ellen Edwards Drechsler

Can't decide if you want a shoulder purse or a hand purse? This bag is for you. Change the length by adjusting the length of the handles.

SIZE
Approx 32 inches around x 9 inches high, after felting

MATERIALS
- Plymouth Outback Wool 100 percent virgin wool worsted weight yarn (370 yds/200g per skein): 2 skeins blue/gray print #901 (A)
- Plymouth Outback Mohair 70 percent mohair/26 percent wool/4 percent nylon bulky weight yarn (218 yds/100g per skein): 3 skeins blue/green multi #801 (B)
- Plymouth Galway 100 percent virgin wool worsted weight yarn (210 yds/100g per skein): 1 skein teal #116 (C)
- Size 13 (9mm) 2 double-pointed needles
- Size 15 (10mm) 32-inch circular needle or size needed to obtain gauge
- Stitch markers

GAUGE
9 sts = 4 inches/10cm in St st with larger needles and 1 strand each of A and B held tog

Row gauge is not critical for this project.

PATTERN NOTES
Purse is worked with 1 strand each of A and B held tog.

Instructions are for a handbag. If you would like a shoulder bag, make each strap longer as directed.

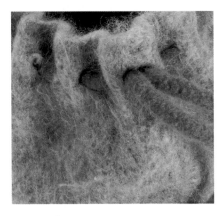

BOTTOM
With 1 strand each of A and B held tog, cast on 10 sts.

Working in garter st, [inc 1 st each end every other row] 8 times. (26 sts)

Work even until piece measures 5 inches above last inc.

[Dec 1 st each end every other row] 8 times. (10 sts)

Begin sides
With 10 sts on RH needle, pm after last st, pick up and knit 48 sts across long side of bottom, 10 sts across cast-on edge, 48 sts across 2nd long side, knit rem 10 sts. (116 sts)

Join; knit every rnd until purse measures 20 inches above picked-up sts.

Eyelet rnd: *K2, bind off next 2 sts; rep from * around.

Next rnd: *K2, cast on 2 sts over bound-off sts of previous row; rep from * around.

Knit 2 rnds.

Dec rnd: *K3, k2tog; rep from to last st, k1. (93 sts)

Bind off.

STRAPS
Make 2
With dpn and C, cast on 4 sts. *K4, sl sts back on LH needle; rep from * until strap measures 72 inches (100 inches if you plan on making a shoulder bag)

Next row: K4tog, fasten off last st.

FELTING

Place purse in old pillowcase and straps in 2nd case.

Place in washer set on Hot Wash with Cold Rinse.

Checking often, run through cycle until desired amount of felting and size are achieved.

As washers, water temperature and other factors vary, you may need to cycle through more than once, or place in dryer to achieve desired effect.

The key to getting the results you want is to **check the piece often.**

Once the desired size is obtained, stuff the purse with plastic bags to shape it while it air dries. Air dry straps if needed.

ASSEMBLY

Weave straps through eyelets, beg and ending at opposite ends of bag.

Tie ends in overhand knot. ■

IT'S A SNAP
SCARF & HAT

Design by Melissa Leapman

Thick yarns and big needles make a warm & comfortable set that's a snap to knit.

SKILL LEVEL
■■□□
EASY

YARN WEIGHT   YARN WEIGHT
(5)   (6)
BULKY   SUPER BULKY
A   B

SIZE
Woman's—One size fits most

FINISHED MEASUREMENTS
Scarf: Approx 7 x 44 inches
Hat circumference: 19 inches

MATERIALS
- Plymouth Outback Mohair 70 percent mohair/26 percent wool/4 percent nylon bulky weight yarn (200 yds/100g per hank): 1 hank each for scarf and hat blue/green multi #801 (A)
- Plymouth Yukon 35 percent mohair/35 percent wool/30 percent acrylic super bulky weight yarn (59 yds/100g per skein): 2 skeins each for scarf and hat light

green #678 (B)
- Size 17 (12.75mm) needles or size needed to obtain gauge

GAUGE
8 sts and 11 rows = 4 inches/10cm in Mistake Rib
To save time, take time to check gauge.

SPECIAL ABBREVIATION
CDD (Centered Double Decrease): Sl 2 sts as if to k2tog, k1, pass 2 slipped sts over k st.

PATTERN STITCH
Mistake Rib (multiple of 4 sts + 3)
All rows: *K2, p2; rep from * to last 3 sts, k2, p1.

PATTERN NOTE
One strand each of A and B are held tog throughout.

SCARF

With 1 strand each of A and B held tog, cast on 15 sts.
Work even in Mistake Rib pat until scarf measures 9 inches from beg.
Divide for slit
Next row: Work across first 7 sts,

join 2nd ball of yarn and bind off center st, work to end row.

Working on both sides of opening with separate balls of yarn, work even until opening measures 4 inches.

Join opening

Work across first section knitting in front and back of last st, work across 2nd section, cutting extra yarn. (15 sts)

Work even until scarf measures 44 inches.

Bind off in pat.

HAT

With 1 strand each of A and B held tog, cast on 39 sts.

Work even in Mistake Rib pat until hat measures 10½ inches from beg.

Shape crown

Row 1 (WS): K2, p1, *CDD, p1; rep from * across. (21 sts)

Row 2: K1, *CDD, k1; rep from * across. (11 sts)

Row 3: P2, *p2tog, p1; rep from * across. (8 sts)

Cut yarn, leaving a long end.

Draw yarn through rem sts twice and pull tightly.

Sew back seam, reversing last 4 inches of seam for cuff.

Turn cuff to right side of hat. ■

GENERAL INFORMATION

BASIC STITCHES

Garter Stitch
On straight needles knit every row. When working in the round on circular or double-pointed needles, knit one round then purl one round.

Stockinette Stitch
On straight needles knit right-side rows and purl wrong-side rows. When working on circular or double-pointed needles, knit all rounds.

Reverse Stockinette Stitch
On straight needles purl right-side rows and knit wrong-side rows. On circular or double-pointed needles, purl all rounds.

Ribbing
Combines knit and purl stitches within a row to give stretch to the garment. Ribbing is most often used for the lower edge of the front and back, the cuffs and neck edge of garments.

The rib pattern is established on the first row. On subsequent rows the knit stitches are knitted and purl stitches are purled to form the ribs.

READING PATTERN INSTRUCTIONS
Before beginning a pattern, look through it to make sure you are familiar with the abbreviations that are used.

Some patterns may be written for more than one size. In this case the smallest size is given first and others are placed in parentheses. When only one number is given, it applies to all sizes.

You may wish to highlight the numbers for the size you are making before beginning. It is also helpful to place a self-adhesive sheet on the pattern to note any changes made while working the pattern.

MEASURING
To measure pieces, lay them flat on a smooth surface. Take the measurement in the middle of the piece. For example, measure the length to the armhole in the center of the front or back piece, not along the outer edge where the edges tend to curve or roll.

GAUGE
The single most important factor in determining the finished size of a knit item is the gauge. Although not as important for flat, one-piece items, it is important when making a clothing item that needs to fit properly.

It is important to make a stitch gauge swatch about 4 inches square with recommended patterns and needles before beginning.

Measure the swatch. If the number of stitches and rows are fewer than indicated under "Gauge" in the pattern, your needles are too large. Try another swatch with smaller-size needles. If the number of stitches and rows are more than indicated under "Gauge" in the pattern, your needles are too small. Try another swatch with larger-size needles.

Continue to adjust needles until correct gauge is achieved.

WORKING FROM CHARTS
When working with more than one color in a row, sometimes a chart is provided to follow the pattern. On the chart each square represents one stitch. A key is given indicating the color or stitch represented by each color or symbol in the box.

When working in rows, odd-numbered rows are usually read from right to left and even-numbered rows from left to right.

Odd-numbered rows represent the right side of the work and are usually knit. Even-numbered rows represent the wrong side and are usually purled.

When working in rounds, every row on the chart is a right-side row, and is read from right to left.

USE OF ZERO
In patterns that include various sizes, zeros are sometimes necessary. For example, k0 (0,1) means if you are making the smallest or middle size, you would do nothing, and if you are making the largest size, you would k1.

GLOSSARY

bind off—used to finish an edge

cast on—process of making foundation stitches used in knitting

decrease—means of reducing the number of stitches in a row

increase—means of adding to the number of stitches in a row

intarsia—method of knitting a multicolored pattern into the fabric

knitwise—insert needle into stitch as if to knit

make 1—method of increasing using the strand between the last stitch worked and the next stitch

place marker—placing a purchased marker or loop of contrasting yarn onto the needle for ease in working a pattern repeat

purlwise—insert needle into stitch as if to purl

right side—side of garment or piece that will be seen when worn

selvage stitch—edge stitch used to make seaming easier

slip, slip, knit—method of decreasing by moving stitches from left needle to right needle and working them together

slip stitch—an unworked stitch slipped from left needle to right needle, usually as if to purl

wrong side—side that will be inside when garment is worn

work even—continue to work in the pattern as established without working any increases or decreases

work in pattern as established—continue to work following the pattern stitch as it has been set up or established on the needle, working any increases or decreases in such a way that the established pattern remains the same

yarn over—method of increasing by wrapping the yarn over the right needle without working a stitch

Skill Levels

◀☐☐☐
BEGINNER
Projects for first-time knitters using basic knit and purl stitches. Minimal shaping.

◀■☐☐
EASY
Projects using basic stitches, repetitive stitch patterns, simple color changes and simple shaping and finishing.

◀■■☐
INTERMEDIATE
Projects with a variety of stitches, such as basic cables and lace, simple intarsia, double-pointed needles and knitting in the round needle techniques, mid-level shaping and finishing. Projects using

◀■■■
EXPERIENCED
advanced techniques and stitches, such as short rows, Fair Isle, more intricate intarsia, cables, lace patterns and numerous color changes.

Standard Abbreviations

[ ] work instructions within brackets as many times as directed

( ) work instructions within parentheses in the place directed

** repeat instructions following the asterisks as directed

* repeat instructions following the single asterisk as directed

" inch(es)

approx approximately

beg begin/beginning

CC contrasting color

ch chain stitch

cm centimeter(s)

cn cable needle

dec decrease/decreases/decreasing

dpn(s) double-pointed needle(s)

g gram

inc increase/increases/increasing

k knit

k2tog knit 2 stitches together

LH left hand

lp(s) loop(s)

m meter(s)

M1 make one stitch

MC main color

mm millimeter(s)

oz ounce(s)

p purl

pat(s) pattern(s)

p2tog purl 2 stitches together

psso pass slipped stitch over

rem remain/remaining

rep repeat(s)

rev St st reverse stockinette stitch

RH right hand

rnd(s) rounds

RS right side

skp slip, knit, pass stitch over—one stitch decreased

sk2p slip 1, knit 2 together, pass slip stitch over the knit 2 together; 2 stitches have been decreased

sl slip

sl 1k slip 1 knitwise

sl 1p slip 1 purlwise

sl st slip stitch(es)

ssk slip, slip, knit these 2 stitches together—a decrease

ssp slip, slip, purl these 2 stitches together--a decrease

st(s) stitch(es)

St st stockinette stitch/stocking stitch

tbl through back loop(s)

tog together

WS wrong side

wyib with yarn in back

wyif with yarn in front

yd(s) yard(s)

yfwd yarn forward

yo yarn over

Changing Yarn Colors

CARRYING YARNS

There are a few tricks to changing colors when knitting. When colors are changed every so many rows at the beginning of the row, it is often easier to carry the yarn along the edge, than to weave in all the ends after completing the project. When changing colors, bring the previous color from below over the working color then start the row as usual, Photo A.

When colors of yarn are

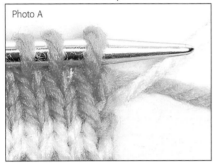

Photo A

changed within the row they are carried along the wrong side of the work and twisted around each other as the pattern is worked. This single twist prevents holes from appearing in the work where colors are changed.

The photos B and C show the twist from the right side and the wrong side.

This same twisting technique can also be used when a yarn is

Photo B

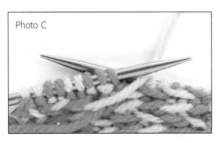

Photo C

carried over a large number of stitches. Every three or four stitches, bring the carried yarn around the working yarn to hold it in place and eliminate long strands of yarn across the wrong side of the work.

INTARSIA

In certain patterns there are larger areas of color within the piece. Since this type of pattern requires a new color only for that section, it is not necessary to carry the yarn back and forth across the back. For this type of color change, a separate ball of yarn or bobbin is used for each color, making the yarn available only where needed. The yarns are twisted in the same manner but are not carried across the entire wrong side of the work.

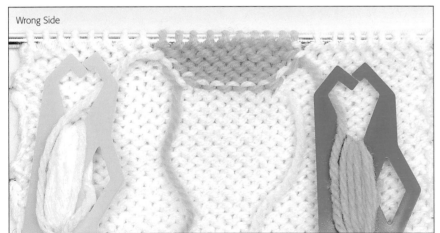

Wrong Side

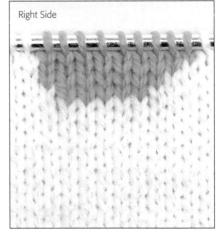

Right Side

Cables

Cable needles are used to hold stitches either in front or in back of the work and out of the way while other stitches are worked. They are made with a point at both ends so stitches can be slipped on at one end and worked off at the other. Some cable needles have a curved area in the middle to hold the stitches so they won't slip off.

TWISTING THE CABLE

A cable can be twisted with any number of stitches. The following illustrates a cable worked over six stitches. Half of the stitches are held behind the work on a cable needle while the other stitches are being worked. Then the stitches on the cable needle are worked. This changes the order of the stitches and forms a cable.

Slip next three stitches onto cable needle and hold in back of work. (Photo A) Knit next three stitches from left-hand needle. Knit three stitches from cable needle to complete the cable twist.

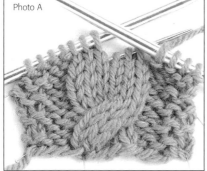

Photo A

Photo B

Twisting the cable by holding the stitches in the back each time creates a cable that twists to the right. (Photo B)

To twist the cable to the left, slip the next three stitches onto a cable needle and hold the stitches in front of the work. (Photo C) Knit the next three stitches. Knit the stitches from the cable needle to complete the cable twist.

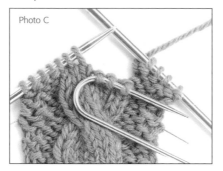

Photo C

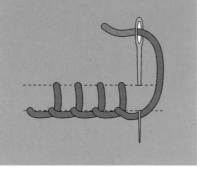

Photo D

Holding the stitches in the front each time results in a cable that twists to the left. (Photo D)

BLANKET STITCH

This stitch is worked along edge of piece. Bring needle up and make a counterclockwise loop. Take stitch as indicated, keeping the thread beneath the point of needle. Pull through to form stitch. Continue in same manner around outer edge.

Zipper How-To

Zippers can easily be added to a knit garment. Different weights of garments need different-weight zippers. Heavy separating zippers are used on jackets and cardigans, while regular dressmaking zippers are used for neck or skirt openings.

The zipper should be sewn in by hand using a backstitch through both the zipper and knit piece.

To add a zipper, place the knit edges over the zipper so the zipper teeth are covered and the seam is centered over the zipper. From the right side, pin in place.

On the wrong side, tack the edges of the zipper to the garment. Turn to the right side and backstitch the zipper in place.

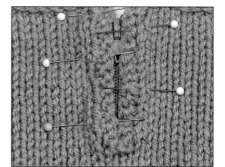

SEAM FINISHES

MATTRESS SEAM

This type of seam can be used for vertical seams (like side seams). It is worked with the right sides of the pieces facing you, making it easier to match stitches for stripe patterns. It is worked between the first and second stitch at the edge of the piece and works best when the first stitch is a selvage stitch.

To work this seam, thread a tapestry needle with matching yarn. Insert the needle into one corner of work from back to front, just above the cast-on stitch, leaving a 3-inch tail. Take needle to edge of other piece and bring it from back to front at the corner of this piece.

Return to the first piece and insert the needle from the right to wrong side where the thread comes out of the piece. Slip the needle upward under two horizontal threads and bring the needle through to the right side.

Cross to the other side and repeat the same process "down where you came out, under two threads and up."

Continue working back and forth on the two pieces in the same manner for about an inch, then gently pull on the thread pulling the two pieces together. (Photo A)

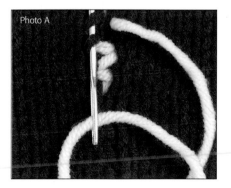

Photo A

Complete the seam and fasten off. Use the beginning tail to even-up the lower edge by working a figure 8 between the cast-on stitches at the corners. Insert the threaded needle

from front to back under both threads of the corner cast-on stitch on the edge opposite the tail, then into the same stitch on the first edge. Pull gently until the "8" fills the gap. (Photo B)

Photo B

When a project is made with a textured yarn that will not pull easily through the pieces, it is recommended that a smooth yarn of the same color be used to work the seam.

GARTER STITCH SEAMS

The "bumps" of the garter stitch selvage nestle between each other in a garter stitch seam, often producing a nearly reversible seam. This is a good seam for afghan strips and blocks of the same color. Starting as for the mattress seam, work from bump to bump, alternating sides. In this case you enter each stitch only once.

MATCHING PATTERNS

When it comes to matching stripes and other elements in a sweater design, a simple formula makes things line up perfectly: Begin the seam in the usual way.

Enter the first stitch of each new color stripe (or pattern detail) on the same side as you began the seam, the same side as your tail is hanging.

Twisted Cord

Items sometimes require a cord as a drawstring closing or strap. The number of lengths and weight of yarn determine the thickness of the cord.

To form the cord, hold the number of cords indicated together matching ends. Attach one end to a doorknob or hook. Twist the other end in one direction until the length is tightly twisted and begins to kink.

Sometimes the lengths are folded in half before twisting. In this case the loose ends are attached to the doorknob and a pencil is slipped into the folded loop at the other end. Turn the pencil to twist the cord.

Once the cord is tightly twisted, continue to hold the twisted end while folding the yarn in the middle. Remove the end from the knob or hook and match the two ends, then release them allowing the cord to twist on itself.

Trim the cord ends to the desired length and knot each end. If the cord is woven through eyelets, it may be necessary to tie a second knot in the end to prevent it from slipping back through the eyelet opening.

3-Needle Bind Off

Use this technique for seaming two edges together, such as when joining a shoulder seam. Hold the edge stitches on two separate needles with right sides together.

With a third needle, knit together a stitch from the front needle with one from the back.

Repeat, knitting a stitch from the front needle with one from the back needle once more.

Slip the first stitch over the second.

Repeat knitting, a front and back pair of stitches together, then bind one off.

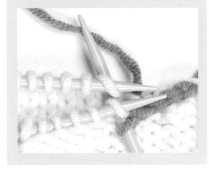

FRINGE

Cut a piece of cardboard half as long as specified in instructions for strands plus ½ inch for trimming. Wind yarn loosely and evenly around cardboard. When cardboard is filled, cut yarn across one end. Do this several times then begin fringing. Wind additional strands as necessary.

SINGLE KNOT FRINGE

Hold specified number of strands for one knot together, fold in half. Hold project to be fringed with right side facing you. Use crochet hook to draw folded end through space or stitch indicated from right to wrong side.

Pull loose ends through folded section.

Draw knot up firmly. Space

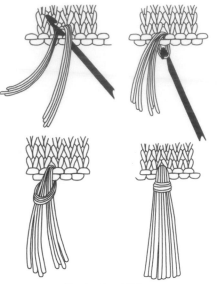

Single Knot Fringe

knots as indicated in pattern instructions.

DOUBLE KNOT FRINGE

Begin by working Single Knot Fringe completely across one end of piece. With right side facing you and working from left to right, take half the strands of one knot and half the strands of the knot next to it and knot them together.

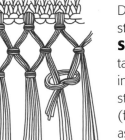

Double Knot Fringe

TRIPLE KNOT FRINGE

Work Double Knot Fringe across. On the right side, work from left to right tying a third row of knots.

Triple Knot Fringe

SPAGHETTI FRINGE

Following Single Knot Fringe instructions, tie each knot with just one strand of yarn.

Kitchener Stitch

This method of weaving with two needles is used for the toes of socks and flat seams. To weave the edges together and form an unbroken line of stockinette stitch, divide all stitches evenly onto two knitting needles—one behind the other. Thread yarn into tapestry needle. Hold needles with wrong sides together and work from right to left as follows:

Step 1: Insert tapestry needle into first stitch on front needle as to purl. Draw yarn through stitch, leaving stitch on knitting needle.

Step 2: Insert tapestry needle into the first stitch on the back needle as to purl. Draw yarn through stitch and slip stitch off knitting needle.

Step 3: Insert tapestry needle into the next stitch on same (back) needle as to knit, leaving stitch on knitting needle.

Step 4: Insert tapestry needle into the first stitch on the front needle as to knit. Draw yarn through stitch and slip stitch off knitting needle.

Step 5: Insert tapestry needle into the next stitch on same (front) needle as to purl. Draw yarn through stitch, leaving stitch on knitting needle.

Repeat Steps 2 through 5 until one stitch is left on each needle. Then repeat Steps 2 and 4. Fasten off. Woven stitches should be the same size as adjacent knitted stitches.

KNITTING BASICS

CAST ON

Leaving an end about an inch long for each stitch to be cast on, make a slip knot on the right needle.

Place the thumb and index finger of your left hand between the yarn ends with the long yarn end over your thumb and the strand from the skein over your index finger. Close your other fingers over the strands to hold them against your palm. Spread your thumb and index fingers apart and draw the yarn into a "V."

Place the needle in front of the strand around your thumb and bring it underneath this strand. Carry the needle over and under the strand on your index finger.

Draw through loop on thumb.

Drop the loop from your thumb and draw up the strand to form a stitch on the needle.

Repeat until you have cast on the number of stitches indicated in the pattern. Remember to count the beginning slip knot as a stitch.

CABLE CAST-ON

This type of cast-on is used when adding stitches in the middle or at the end of a row.

Make a slip knot on the left needle.

Knit a stitch in this knot and place it on the left needle.

Insert the right needle between the last two stitches on the left needle. Knit a stitch and place it on the left needle. Repeat for each stitch needed.

KNIT (K)

Insert tip of right needle from front to back in next stitch on left needle.

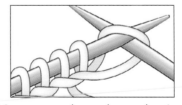

Bring yarn under and over the tip of the right needle.

Pull yarn loop through the stitch with right needle point.

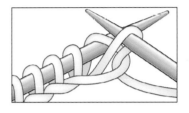

Slide the stitch off the left needle. The new stitch is on the right needle.

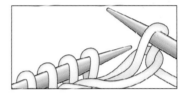

PURL (P)

With yarn in front, insert tip of right needle from back to front through next stitch on the left needle.

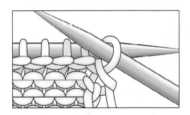

Bring yarn around the right needle counterclockwise.

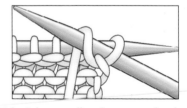

With right needle, draw yarn back through the stitch.

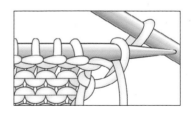

Slide the stitch off the left needle. The new stitch is on the right needle.

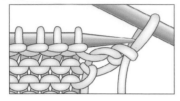

BIND OFF
Binding off (knit)

Knit first two stitches on left needle. Insert tip of left needle into first stitch worked on right needle and pull it over the second stitch and completely off the needle.

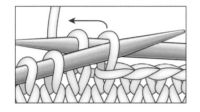

Knit the next stitch and repeat. When one stitch remains on right needle, cut yarn and draw tail through last stitch to fasten off.

Binding off (purl)

Purl first two stitches on left needle. Insert tip of left needle into first stitch worked on right needle and pull it over the second stitch and completely off the needle.

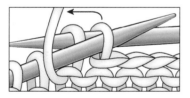

Purl the next stitch and repeat. When one stitch remains on right needle, cut yarn and draw tail through last stitch to fasten off.

INCREASE (INC)
Two stitches in one stitch
Increase (knit)

Knit the next stitch in the usual manner, but don't remove the stitch from the left needle. Place right needle behind left needle

and knit again into the back of the same stitch. Slip original stitch off left needle.

Increase (purl)

Purl the next stitch in the usual manner, but don't remove the stitch from the left needle. Place right needle behind left needle and purl again into the back of the same stitch. Slip original stitch off left needle.

INVISIBLE INCREASE (M1)

There are several ways to make or increase one stitch.

Make 1 with Left Twist (M1L)

Insert left needle from front to back under the horizontal loop between the last stitch worked and next stitch on left needle.

With right needle, knit into the back of this loop.

To make this increase on the purl side, insert left needle in same manner and purl into the back of the loop.

Make 1 with Right Twist (M1R)

Insert left needle from back to front under the horizontal loop between the last stitch worked and next stitch on left needle.

With right needle, knit into the front of this loop.

To make this increase on the purl side, insert left needle in same manner and purl into the front of the loop.

Make 1 with Backward Loop over the right needle

With your thumb, make a loop over the right needle.

Slip the loop from your thumb onto the needle and pull to tighten.

Make 1 in top of stitch below

Insert tip of right needle into the stitch on left needle one row below.

Knit this stitch, then knit the stitch on the left needle.

DECREASE (DEC)
Knit 2 together (k2tog)
Put tip of right needle through next two stitches on left needle as to knit. Knit these two stitches as one.

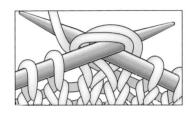

Purl 2 together (p2tog)
Put tip of right needle through next two stitches on left needle as to purl. Purl these two stitches as one.

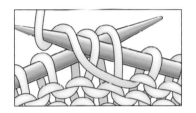

SLIP, SLIP, KNIT (SSK)
Slip next two stitches, one at a time, as to knit from left needle to right needle.

Insert left needle in front of both stitches and work off needle together.

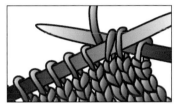

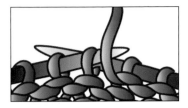

Slip, Slip, Purl (ssp)
Slip next two stitches, one at a time, as to knit from left needle to right needle. Slip these stitches back onto left needle keeping them twisted.

Purl these two stitches together through back loops.

CROCHET BASICS

Some knit items are finished with a crochet trim or edging. Below are some abbreviations used in crochet and a review of some basic crochet stitches.

CROCHET ABBREVIATIONS

ch	chain stitch
dc	double crochet
hdc	half double crochet
lp(s)	loop(s)
sc	single crochet
sl st	slip stitch
yo	yarn over

Chain Stitch (ch)
Begin by making a slip knot on the hook. Bring the yarn over the hook from back to front and draw through the loop on the hook.

For each additional chain stitch, bring the yarn over the hook from back to front and draw through the loop on the hook.

Single Crochet (sc)
Insert the hook in the second chain through the center of the V. Bring the yarn over the hook from back to front.

Draw the yarn through the chain stitch and onto the hook.

Again bring yarn over the hook from back to front and draw it through both loops on hook.

For additional rows of single crochet, insert the hook under both loops of the previous stitch instead of through the center of the V as when working into the chain stitch.

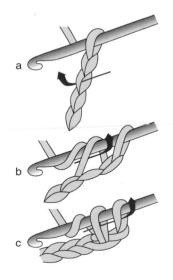

Reverse Single Crochet (reverse sc)

Working from left to right, insert hook under both loops of the next stitch to the right.

Bring yarn over hook from back to front and draw through both loops on hook.

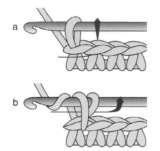

Half-Double Crochet (hdc)

Bring yarn over hook from back to front, insert hook in indicated chain stitch.

Draw yarn through the chain stitch and onto the hook.

Bring yarn over the hook from back to front and draw it through all three loops on the hook in one motion.

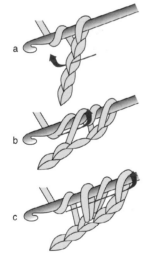

Double crochet (dc)

Yo, insert hook in st, yo, pull through st, (yo, pull through 2 lps) 2 times.

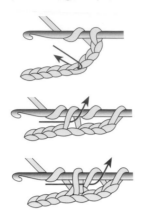

Treble crochet (tr)

Yo 2 times, insert hook in st, yo, pull through st, (yo, pull through 2 lps) 3 times.

Slip Stitch (sl st)

Insert hook under both loops of the stitch, bring yarn over the hook from back to front and draw it through the stitch and the loop on the hook.

Picot

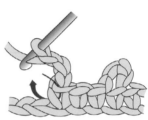

Picots can be made in a variety of ways so refer to pattern for specific instructions.

Chain required number of stitches. Insert hook at base of chain stitches and through back loop of stitch, complete as indicated in pattern. ■

INCHES INTO MILLIMETERS & CENTIMETERS (Rounded off slightly)

inches	mm	cm	inches	cm	inches	cm	inches	cm
1/8	3	0.3	5	12.5	21	53.5	38	96.5
1/4	6	0.6	5 1/2	14	22	56	39	99
3/8	10	1	6	15	23	58.5	40	101.5
1/2	13	1.3	7	18	24	61	41	104
5/8	15	1.5	8	20.5	25	63.5	42	106.5
3/4	20	2	9	23	26	66	43	109
7/8	22	2.2	10	25.5	27	68.5	44	112
1	25	2.5	11	28	28	71	45	114.5
1 1/4	32	3.2	12	30.5	29	73.5	46	117
1 1/2	38	3.8	13	33	30	76	47	119.5
1 3/4	45	4.5	14	35.5	31	79	48	122
2	50	5	15	38	32	81.5	49	124.5
2 1/2	65	6.5	16	40.5	33	84	50	127
3	75	7.5	17	43	34	86.5		
3 1/2	90	9	18	46	35	89		
4	100	10	19	48.5	36	91.5		
4 1/2	115	11.5	20	51	37	94		

KNITTING NEEDLES CONVERSION CHART

U.S.	0	1	2	3	4	5	6	7	8	9	10	10 1/2	11	13	15
Metric(mm)	2	2 1/4	2 3/4	3 1/4	3 1/2	3 3/4	4	4 1/2	5	5 1/2	6	6 1/2	8	9	10

CROCHET HOOKS CONVERSION CHART

U.S.	1/B	2/C	3/D	4/E	5/F	6/G	8/H	9/I	10/J	10 1/2/K	N
Continental-mm	2.25	2.75	3.25	3.5	3.75	4.25	5	5.5	6	6.5	9.0

Standard Yarn Weight System

Categories of yarn, gauge ranges, and recommended needle sizes

Yarn Weight Symbol & Category Names	1 SUPER FINE	2 FINE	3 LIGHT	4 MEDIUM	5 BULKY	6 SUPER BULKY
Type of Yarns in Category	Sock, Fingering, Baby	Sport, Baby	DK, Light Worsted	Worsted, Afghan, Aran	Chunky, Craft, Rug	Bulky, Roving
Knit Gauge* Ranges in Stockinette Stitch to 4 inches	21–32 sts	23–26 sts	21–24 sts	16–20 sts	12–15 sts	6–11 sts
Recommended Needle in Metric Size Range	2.25–3.25mm	3.25–3.75mm	3.75–4.5mm	4.5–5.5mm	5.5–8mm	8mm
Recommended Needle U.S. Size Range	1 to 3	3 to 5	5 to 7	7 to 9	9 to 11	11 and larger

* GUIDELINES ONLY: The above reflect the most commonly used gauges and needle sizes for specific yarn categories.

SPECIAL THANKS

We would like to thank Plymouth Yarn Co. for providing all the yarn used in this book. We really appreciate the help provided by their staff, especially JoAnne Turcotte, throughout the publishing process. It's been great working with them. We also thank the talented designers whose work is featured in this collection.

Anita Closic
Tropical Paradise Throw & Pillow, 14
Make Me Smile Ensemble, 132

Gayle Bunn
Woven for Warmth Afghan, 23
Easy-to-Wear Lush Tunic, 87
Rainbows in the Snow Capelet, 110
For You & Your Pampered
    Pooch, 146
Paint the Town, 150

Ellen Edwards Drechsler
Claudia's Felted Purse With
    Scarf, 158
Edith's Felted Drawstring Bag, 160

Lanie Hering
Take Notice Pillows, 26

Melissa Leapman
Celtic Knot Pullover, 83
Evening Glitz Jacket, 91
It's a Snap Scarf & Hat, 162

Katharine Hunt
Evening at Home Throw, 28
Check-In for Fun Hoodie Pullover, 71
First Class Leisure Pullover, 67
Very Easy, Very Cozy Ruana, 113

Celeste Pinheiro
Bright & Cheery Baby Set, 50
Mom's Casual Cable Cardigan, 43
Dog's Cable Comfort Sweater, 56
Kid's Classic Cable Pullover, 46
Snowtime Cable Scarf, 54
Relaxed & Warm Lattice Pullover, 99
Zip Hoodie for Active Boys, 104
Good Times Hat & Scarf, 154

Cindy Polfer
Easy Elongated Stitch Poncho, 124
Tie One on: 1 Stitch, 4 Ways, 135
Fluff With Style, 156

Laura Polley
Twist the Night Away Afghan, 17
Everyone Loves Diamonds
    Afghan, 31
Flying Colors Felted Rug &
    Pillow, 34

Pauline Schultz
Trading Post Rug & Pillow, 8
Sky's the Limit Jacket, 79
Spice-Up-Your-Wardrobe Shawl, 116

Colleen Smitherman
Merriment Mittens for One &
    All, 140

Kennita Tully
Make Mine Colorful Throw, 12
Mom's Special Outing Cardigan, 59
Daughter's Special Outing
    Cardigan, 64
So Precious Child's A-Line Jacket, 95

Barbara Venishnick
Fun & Furry Sweater Jacket, 75
Peruvian Lace Cable Shawl, 119

Kathy Wesley
Truly Toasty Classic Poncho, 126
Fashionable, Fringed Girl's
    Poncho, 128

Lois S. Young
Over or Under Reversible Afghan, 20
Go-With-Everything Poncho, 122

Diane Zangl
Warm Pleasures Hat, Wristers &
    Scarf, 143